Emma Ineson is the Bishop of Penrith in the Diocese of Carlisle. She spent most of her childhood in Kenya, East Africa, before moving to the 'land of her mothers', the Welsh Valleys, for her teenage years. She studied English at Birmingham University, including an MPhil on the metaphors used in the ordination of women debates, and a PhD on the language of worship. It was reading the stories of women called to ordained ministry for her studies that first began to awaken in her a sense of her own calling.

Emma and her husband Mat trained together for ordination at Trinity College, Bristol, prior to a job-share curacy in Sheffield and four years as chaplains to the Lee Abbey community in Devon.

Emma joined the faculty at Trinity College in 2007 as Tutor in Practical Theology, eventually becoming Director of Practical Training. From 2013 to 2014, she worked for a year as Chaplain to the then Bishop of Bristol, Mike Hill, before returning to Trinity College as its Principal. In 2016, she was appointed as an Honorary Chaplain to the Queen. She has been a member of General Synod of the Church of England, the Faith and Order Commission, the Implementation and Dialogue Group on the Five Guiding Principles and the Lambeth Conference 2020 Design Group. She is Chair of the Council of Reference of CPAS and Central Chaplain to the Mothers' Union.

Mat is a parish priest and mission enabler in Cumbria. They have two adult children and two black dogs.

AMBITION

What Jesus said about power, success
and counting stuff

Emma Ineson

First published in Great Britain in 2019

Society for Promoting Christian Knowledge
36 Causton Street
London SW1P 4ST
www.spck.org.uk

British Library Cataloguing-in-Publication Data
A catalogue record for this book is available from the British Library

ISBN 978-0-281-08012-0
eBook ISBN 978-0-281-08013-7

1 3 5 7 9 10 8 6 4 2

Typeset by Manila Typesetting Company
First printed in Great Britain by Jellyfish Print Solutions
Subsequently digitally reprinted in Great Britain

eBook by Manila Typesetting Company

Produced on paper from sustainable forests

Contents

Foreword

When Bishop Emma was kind enough to ask me to write this foreword, I reflected on my own notions and experience of leadership. I might look highly qualified in the subject of leadership, but that qualification does not come as a result of any particular knowledge or skill; rather, it comes through my many mistakes in many different roles. I have learnt that in leadership and leaders, humility is paramount, motivation is key and a good sense of humour, as Bishop Emma knows so well and displays so splendidly in this book, is, perhaps above all else, vital.

As Christians, we often want to make a difference. We want to see the world changed. Yet, at the very beginning of the Christian faith, Christ didn't look successful at all. He was crucified, suffering the shame and ignominy of a criminal's death, mocked by his detractors and leaving his supporters despairing. You may well ask (and many did, and do), 'Where was the success in that? Where was the leadership?' Christ teaches us that everything we thought about victory and power was wrong. With Christ's death and resurrection, the meaning of success isn't the same any more – it is not about personal glory, it is about the glory of God.

This book is a wonderful reminder, for both people who our society thinks of as being in 'positions of power' and those whose power and leadership we don't always recognize but is nonetheless so important, that power and success come in many different forms and ways. From the power of a bishop leading his or her flock, to the parishioner who cares for fellow Christians, to the power of the seemingly helpless Christ on the cross, when successful, they all hold in common that their ambition is for the glory of God, found when we do not seek the credit for ourselves or our own advantage. I am reminded of Cranmer's words in one of the collects, 'in whose service is perfect freedom'. Those who serve will invariably find themselves liberated in their leadership.

We should be ambitious in putting, as Bishop Emma phrases it, our whole hearts into doing God's will and bringing about God's kingdom. But we should acknowledge that this will probably not look like what we expect. Our project is, ultimately, an eternal one and our success will be in the bringing closer of the Kingdom of Heaven – which is as small as a mustard seed, led by humble fishermen, with a crucified Lord. Once we have accepted that results are in God's hands, plant the seeds and you may count on God to water them.

So look for power in those you wouldn't expect. Appreciate the ambition of those whose goals look very different from yours. Acknowledge the leadership and talents of the person you think you should be leading you. And see the success in those who look like they have failed. Turn your face to God, in the understanding that, as Matthew 20.16 tells us, 'So the last shall be first, and the first last'. And read Bishop Emma's book, be encouraged by her advice and inspired by her wisdom and humour.

Justin Welby
The Archbishop of Canterbury

Acknowledgements

This book has been forming for a very long time, mostly during my 12 years on the staff of Trinity College, Bristol, and especially during the latter five years as its principal. I am grateful to students past and present who taught me so much about how to 'live like the kingdom is near', and how to grow and laugh and love and learn in community. Anything I am able to say about leadership has come about through wrestling with the issues with my colleagues, and I thank them for their forbearance and inspiration, especially Andrew Lucas, whose friendship, wisdom and humour have made life and leadership so much more enjoyable than it otherwise would be. Thank you to those people who, over the years, have noticed and nurtured godly ambition in me: John Perry, Chris Turner, Marlene Parsons, Rachel Treweek, Jackie Searle, Jane Williams, John Nolland, David Williams, Chris Edmondson, David Wenham, John Dunnett, Rich Johnson, Kate Wharton, Ian Parkinson, James Lawrence, Christine Froude, David Hoyle, Mike Hill and James Newcome. Without the encouragement of everyone at SPCK, this book would not have seen the light of day; thanks especially to Alison Barr, Sam Richardson, Elizabeth Neep, Michelle Clark and Carnie Walker. I am so grateful to my wonderful parents, Tony and Barbara, whose unfailing support has been the hidden answer to that oft-asked question, 'Goodness, how do you manage to do all that?' Above all, thanks to my darling Mat and our superb children Molly and Toby. I couldn't be more proud of you.

1

Success and failure

Do not be fobbed off with mere personal success or
acceptance. You will make all kinds of mistakes; but as
long as you are generous and true, and also fierce, you
cannot hurt the world or even seriously distress her.
(Winston Churchill)[1]

If I had a message to my contemporaries it is surely this:
Be anything you like, be madmen, drunks, and bastards
of every shape and form, but at all costs avoid one thing:
success. . . . If you are too obsessed with success, you will
forget to live.
(Thomas Merton)[2]

Two key moments have informed the writing of this book.

The first moment. I am in the kitchen cooking the family
tea (dinner, if you're from the south of England). My husband
walks in. He's a Church of England vicar. He's a very good
Church of England vicar. He's vicar of a very good Church
of England church. His church has just been grouped with
four other churches in the local area to form a 'Mission Area'.
His church is to be the 'Resourcing Church'. The idea behind
this is that these five churches will do things together, pool
resources, think Big Thoughts about mission and set out to
change the world for Jesus. It's a very good plan. So good that

it has been granted Strategic Development Funding (every one of those words scares me a little bit). This amounts to Quite a Lot of Money that is to be used to pump resources into the churches (he gets an associate minister as part of the team, paid for from these funds), so that the churches will have an impact on their local communities and, hopefully, grow.

In return for this Quite a Lot of Money, everything must be measured and accounted for. Growth must be tracked and monitored. My husband goes to lots of meetings with Important People from the Diocese and beyond, where words like 'goals', 'outcomes', 'dials' and 'dashboard' are used. A consequence of getting Quite a Lot of Money is that now his every move is being watched. And on the day concerned, the day on which I am in the kitchen cooking tea and he walks in, a set of measurements has come in that shows the churches aren't growing in numbers quite as much or as fast as they were expected to. The figures for that particular month are not quite as they should be. He tells me about this latest set of statistics. This is not the moment in itself. The moment is when I see written on his face what these numbers are doing to his soul. He is a bright, able, confident man, passionate about the mission of God in the world. People love him and he loves people. He loves Jesus and his churches and has given his life to serving them. He reveals Christ to them. He is a Very Good Vicar. Yet, I see in that moment glimpses of self-doubt and disappointment that should never have been part of this journey.

The Church of England, the part of the Church of which I am a part and I know most closely, has set out on an ambitious programme of growth and revitalization. At the start of his tenure, the Archbishop of Canterbury Justin Welby set as one of his goals (along with prayer, reconciliation and the religious life) evangelism and witness: 'Evangelism is joining in the work of God to bring redemption to this world. It's proclaiming the revolution of love that has rescued God's world from darkness to light.'[3] Can't argue with that. The Archbishop's website says that:

> We aren't committed to evangelism because we are scared the Church is dying. We don't make known his love because we want to look successful. We announce what God has done in Christ because we are compelled by his love. Everybody must be told.

Amen, amen.

New initiatives and strategies for Church growth have been developed because of this priority of witness. The ambitious Renewal and Reform programme, 'aimed at *helping us become a growing Church* for all people and for all places',[4] is designed to streamline efficiency in the Church of England and remove barriers to Church growth. It has three main priorities: to contribute as the national Church to the common good, to facilitate the *growth* of the Church in numbers and depth of discipleship, and to reimagine the Church's ministry. The web page says that it:

> prayerfully hopes to see a *growing* Church as fruit of all these labours, *growth* understood in its fullest sense . . . One of the clear and intended outcomes of this work is to reverse the decline of the Church of England so that *we*

3

become a growing Church, in every region and for every generation.[5]

Growth is very clearly the order of the day.

And why not? All this is very good and very exciting. Dioceses, such as London, that have embraced these changes have seen a reversal in the downward trend of church attendance and a revitalization of the spiritual life of their communities. This is excellent.

But is there a price to pay?

The Dean of Christ Church, Oxford, Martyn Percy has been a fierce critic of some of the developments. In a speech on clergy well-being to the Annual General Meeting of the charity Sons and Friends of the Clergy,[6] he said that clergy stress is 'fuelled by anxiety about growth and organisation and professionalism'. Percy berated the Church's current focus on 'blue-sky, visionary' thinking and 'aims, objectives and outcomes.'[7] He is not alone in voicing his opposition to what is perceived by some as a trend toward excessive managerialism in the Church, and to the borrowing of the language of goals and targets from the world of leadership, business and management. In a sermon to commemorate former Provost of Southwark David Edwards, the current Dean of Southwark Andrew Nunn lamented the training now required of senior leaders in the Church of England: 'It's leadership and governance and management and financial reporting and targets that are the skill set of the Church today; it's evaluation and peer review that set the standards for what we do.'[8]

What if you agree with our eminent deans that the Church has gone somewhat too far down the road of corporate thinking, yet you are excited about the new opportunities for intentional and strategic growth in mission across our nation? Perhaps you think the deans have got a point, yet you also think that the time has come for us to use all the resources at our disposal, including those borrowed from the so-called secular arena. This book is for those who are keen to be part of the new emphasis on mission and growth in the Church, who resonate with the Archbishop's vision to see numbers heading in the right direction, who welcome a loosening of the structures and strictures of our former traditional ways, who rise to the challenge to grow the Church numerically as well as in discipleship and holiness – but who also sense the roaring lion of failure at the door and fear they may not make it. It is also for Christian leaders in any sphere of work – education, business, healthcare, commerce – who, likewise, are not immune from the same kind of pressure continually to grow and improve, yet want to be able to sift the wheat from the chaff when it comes to ways of thinking about such matters.

The second moment – or, rather, series of moments – that informed my thinking on all this came when I found myself appointed to be a bishop in the Church of England. The Suffragan Bishop of Penrith in the Diocese of Carlisle, to be precise. This amuses me somewhat because when I was thinking about writing on the subject of ambition a while ago, I read a very helpful book by Craig Hill dealing with similar issues,[9] in which he too describes setting out to write a book on ambition and, during that process, being 'promoted' to a more senior position, as president of a seminary. I recall noting the rather conflicted emotions that this turn of events caused in him. 'How funny,' I thought at the time and so I set out to write my own book on ambition. Halfway through writing, the same thing happened to me. I responded to a call and, after 12 years in theological education, the last five as principal of Trinity College in Bristol, I found myself about to take up episcopal ministry. This has been wonderful and welcome and I aim to serve the people and churches of Carlisle Diocese and Cumbria with all the passion and conviction that vocation brings, but it also raises in me all sorts of questions about my own ambition: what is it, where is it focused and is it OK for Christians to call themselves ambitious at all?

Why does it feel, when I speak about ambition and success in a Christian context, that it's a bit like I'm swearing? Ambition – like sex – is something Christians don't feel very comfortable talking about – at least not as it relates to us. *Other* people are ambitious, of course – bad, worldly, sinful people – but not us. Sometimes I tell people I'm writing a book (because that's the kind of thing you do at Christian conferences and in the world of theological education) and hope with all my heart they won't ask me what I'm writing on. Or, even worse, ask what the book is about. 'Ambition,' I mumble into my hand, hoping that they will mishear me and think I'm writing on 'vocation' or 'submission' or something else that sounds a bit more holy. 'Pardon?' they say. 'AMBITION,' I blurt out, waiting for that look of confusion, pity and vague amusement to appear on their face. 'And SUCCESS,' I say (I'm on a roll now). 'Oh. How interesting,' they say. ('Who does she think she is?' I assume they think).

But what am I so squeamish about?

Why do notions of ambition and success sit so uncomfortably in a Christian context? As we'll see in the next chapter, ambition in itself is a fairly neutral concept that can take a God-wards slant or otherwise. Also, growth and success are not the preserve of big business when viewed through the lens of the kingdom of God. So we need to ask what is right about ambition for the Christian leader? What did Jesus say about such things? Whether you are a leader in the Church or a Christian living out your vocation as a headteacher, doctor, salesperson, 'creative' or business leader, how do we think theologically about ambition?

This is not a book about Church leadership; it's a book about leadership. The Church is the arena in which I have exercised leadership and with which I am most familiar, so, inevitably, this book will focus on what it means to measure ambition and success in a Church context. But I am aware that many of the issues I raise here affect those in leadership in all walks of life, not just the Church. This is a book for leaders in whatever sphere, who aim to live by the calling and values of Christ; those who recognize ambition in themselves and, on a good day, would even dare to call it godly ambition, but who possibly find themselves caught up in a growing tide of competitiveness and restlessness around notions of success, and who want to remain on the right side of all that stuff. This book is for those just setting out in leadership, full of the joys of spring, as well as for those who have been round the block a few times and have begun to wonder what it's all about, for those under pressure and weary of having to 'talk up' the successes of ministry and leadership.

Until recently, I spent my days as principal of a theological college, Trinity College Bristol, with over 100 gifted younger leaders studying and training to be ministers in the Church, mostly in the Church of England. They grew up during an era in which they have been told that anything is possible. They are the 'Because You're Worth It' generation. Be whatever you want to be. Achieve whatever you put your mind to. I would go so far as to say that many of those students are ambitious. Ambitious for the gospel. Ambitious to see the kingdom of God more fully realized on earth. Ambitious to see the communities changed for the better. Ambitious to see the oppressed set free. Ambitious to see growing churches. I love and bless their passion and enthusiasm, but many of them are in their twenties and thirties and have 20, 30, 40 years of ministry ahead of them. That ministry will have ups and downs, valleys and peaks, successes and failures. How do they stay on the right side of ambition? How do they make sure that their drive and ambition is Jesus-focused and kingdom-shaped?

Ambition, at least according to my dictionary, is simply, 'a strong desire to do or achieve something'; 'desire and determination to achieve success.'[10] 'Success' comes from the Latin word *successus* (literally, *sub* – next to, *cedere* – to move), meaning, 'an advance', 'a coming up', 'to follow after'. There is some interesting research into the study of the etymology of the word 'success' that suggests, when it arrived in popular English usage in the 1530s, it simply meant 'that which happened after something else', as in 'succession'. Success could be either positive or negative. It was only later that it began to take on more positive connotations of achievement.[11]

Both words – ambition and success – therefore, have a fairly neutral frame of reference, at least in their origins, but both have become associated with thrusting, and perhaps ruthless, leadership. For Christians it's even worse. We know that Jesus said things like 'the last shall be first and the first last' and 'blessed are the meek', and Paul exhorted Christians to 'do nothing out of selfish ambition', so we resist all talk of being ambitious as being Worldly and Not Nice. If I were to go into a room full of clergy, for instance, and invite them to stand up if they call themselves ambitious, my bet is that only a few brave souls would do so – or at least not without questioning what I meant by 'ambitious' first. If growth in the kingdom of God, well yes, of course. If personal ambition, well of course not. How vulgar!

Like many things – like sex, money and power – ambition and success can be understood and approached well or understood and approached badly. If we are going to understand what success looks like for a Christian, we need to recognize and name the difficulty of living in a world where, in some circles at least, success is the ultimate aim and goal, while at the same time knowing that we are citizens of another kingdom, the kingdom of heaven, which turns the values of this world – and, therefore, what constitutes a successful life – on its head.

How will we know if we've been successful?

The questions for Christian leaders are these. What does 'success' look like? How will we know when we have achieved it? How do we understand what it means for a Christian to be 'successful'? (You see, I keep having to put that word in inverted commas, so wary am I of how it sounds to you, my dear holy, upright readers.)

I undertook that most recognized and revered form of research – a Google search – and I found a panoply of books on ambition and success: *Millionaire Success Habits: The gateway to wealth and prosperity*; *The Success Principles: How to get from where you are to where you want to be*; *Creating Success through Positive Attitude: The secret of great and successful men and women*. And not only so-called 'secular' books. Under the 'Christian books' heading I found: *Success Secrets of the Bible*; *Pray your Way to the New Year: Experience supernatural favour, divine protection, success, breakthrough and everlasting peace*; *The Key to Successful Christian Ministry*; *The 100 Most Powerful Prayers for Massive Success*; *Achieving Christian Success* and *The Christian Success Diary*. I didn't buy any of them but, had I read them, I have no doubt that they would have given me their version of what 'success' means – financial blessing, career promotion, recognition, fame, achieving happiness, making an impact, answered prayer, healings, Church growth and so on. For others, including people I know living with ongoing illness, hardships and adverse life circumstances, just getting through a day will constitute success. We could say that 'success' is something of a chameleon concept, able to be whatever we want or deem it to be.

G. K. Chesterton wrote a scathing article on books about success (apparently on being asked to endorse one such a book), first published in the *Illustrated London News*, in which he said:

> To begin with, of course, there is no such thing as Success. Or, if you like to put it so, there is nothing that is not successful. That a thing is successful merely means that

it is; a millionaire is successful in being a millionaire and a donkey in being a donkey.[12]

Is 'success' even a valid word to use, especially for Christians? In the chapter that follows, we will be asking the same question of ambition. The Church at the moment is wrestling with what it means to be 'successful' (although it may not use this word). We feel instinctively the conundrum we are caught in – we were put on earth to achieve something, to do something for God, to make a difference, yet we are unable to do anything in our own strength. We know we need to steer clear of worldly understandings of success, we sense that Jesus' reaction to the whole thing might have been similar to G. K. Chesterton's – and yet God made us with drive and ambition and we WANT TO MAKE A DIFFERENCE.

Perhaps this is why there are so many blogs around addressing this issue of managerialism, growth and how to count success. This is why people seem to fall into two main camps – one the one hand, those who love all that stuff and could eat Gantt charts for breakfast and, on the other, those who decry our recent descent into the miry pit of success-focused, economically determined, secular leadership and management theories. Call me an Anglican, but I think there is an element of truth in both.

After all, the Bible is one big success story, isn't it?

God's instruction to humankind, to, 'Be fruitful and multiply, and fill the earth and subdue it; and have dominion over the fish of the sea and over the birds of the air and over every living thing that moves upon the earth' (Genesis 1.28) arguably finds its successful fulfilment at the end of time in the Holy City when God, who now dwells on earth with his people, is able to say:

> It is done! I am the Alpha and the Omega, the beginning and the end. To the thirsty I will give water as a gift from the spring of the water of life. Those who conquer will inherit these things, and I will be their God and they will be my children.
> (Revelation 21.6–7)

The concept of success was not unknown to our heroes and heroines of the Old Testament, where it is usually understood as being about two things only – being in the presence of the Lord God and being obedient to his ways and laws: 'The LORD was with Joseph, and he became a successful man' (Genesis 39.2); 'David had success in all his undertakings; for the LORD was with him' (1 Samuel 18.14). David's words to his son Solomon exhort him to:

> keep the charge of the LORD your God, walking in his ways and keeping his statutes, his commandments, his ordinances, and his testimonies, as it is written in the law of Moses, so that you may prosper in all that you do and wherever you turn.
> (1 Kings 2.3)

To Joshua, God says:

> Only be strong and very courageous, being careful to act in accordance with all the law that my servant Moses

commanded you; do not turn from it to the right hand or to the left, so that you may be successful wherever you go. (Joshua 1.7)

Yet we know that, for all their successes, their stories are also peppered with arrogance, fear, sin and moral failure.

The New Testament writers generally avoid using the language of success. However, as God's kingdom begins to find its reality on earth in the form of the presence of the incarnate Christ and the burgeoning of the body of Christ, the Church, there is very much a sense of forward movement, momentum and achievement, which could be seen as success. For Paul, any notion of success is rooted and grounded in the knowledge of Jesus Christ as his Lord. He speaks of pressing 'on towards the goal for the prize of the heavenly call of God in Christ Jesus' (Philippians 3.14), yet, in human terms, any success he enjoyed was also accompanied by imprisonment, beatings and exile. Outwardly successful in many ways, he considered everything as 'loss' and 'rubbish' because of the surpassing value of knowing Christ Jesus as Lord (see Philippians 3.5–8).

In the following chapters we will return to notions of ambition and success in the Gospels to examine them more closely and, in particular, in the teachings of Jesus. Suffice it to say for now, however, that the Bible narrative does not sit straightforwardly with concepts of success and achievement. There is always a 'Yes, but . . .' when we try to paint a theological picture of what successful Christian living might look like. Success and failure are close bedfellows in the story of God and his people. But that is hardly surprising, for at the crux (literally) of this big story is an event that looked like the very antithesis of success. God's greatest achievement – the single most successful thing that has ever happened in the entire history of humankind – the death of death, the defeat of sin, hell's destruction and the opening of the gateway to life for all people for all time – looked very much like failure. It looked very much like one man, naked, shamed and abandoned by most of his followers, hanging in agony on a wooden cross outside the city.

That's what it looked like.

The success of failure

Consider how many successes in science, the arts, business, sport and technology come riding on the back of years and years of practice, hard graft, trying, failing and trying again. In 2018, the England football team had a period of (relative) success in the FIFA World Cup, reaching the semi-finals for the first time since 1990. Much was written about the leadership style of then England manager Gareth Southgate, who, it is said, drew on the experience of his own crucial missed penalty in the 1996 World Cup to encourage his young squad not to be terrified of getting it wrong and, therefore, to be willing to take risks. He had missed that penalty and still ended up as England manager, he said, so they too could risk making mistakes without fear that it would blight their prospects, leading to more exciting and, ultimately, successful play. The phrase 'failing forwards' has been coined to describe this kind of learning from mistakes that leads to future success.

It is all too easy to be simplistic about such things, of course. Sometimes failure is deeply harmful and it is by no means clear that any subsequent successes are worth it. In the field of psychiatry, for example, some of our current knowledge about the brain was discovered by means of some truly dreadful, cruel, 'failed' experiments on real people, which caused great suffering. Not all failure is good. The ends do not always justify the means, and we need to think carefully about what we mean by failure. Some failure destroys lives.

Perhaps it is better to say that there are different kinds of failure and different kinds of potential for learning from them. Amy Edmondson, Professor of Leadership and Management at Harvard Business School, in her fascinating book about developing 'psychological safety' in the workplace, writes of the need to encourage the admission of failure in order to release future fearless experimentation and risk-taking, which is the root of innovation.[13] She acknowledges, however, that not all failure is to be encouraged or welcomed, and that failure can be ranked on a scale from 'vital to get it right' (medical procedures, for example) to 'necessary to find out new things' (pushing the boundaries of innovation). She suggests a basic typology of failure types, from preventable failure (deviations from known processes that produce unwanted outcomes), to intelligent failure (novel forays into new territory leading to new outcomes). She concludes, 'Successful failure is an art. It helps if you can fail at the right time and for the right reasons.'[14]

Successful failure is an essential component of successful leadership, which involves an accompanying willingness to acknowledge and embrace vulnerability and weakness. Hence, Paul can state, 'On behalf of such a one I will boast, but on my own behalf I will not boast, except of my weaknesses' (2 Corinthians 12.5). Gregory the Great in his *Pastoral Rule* (a kind of leadership book for sixth-century clergy) echoes these sentiments: 'whatever works are brought to perfection, consideration of our own infirmity should depress us with regard to them, lest the swelling of elation distinguish even them before the eyes of hidden judgement.'[15] Somewhat more recently, Brené Brown describes the particular benefits of acknowledging vulnerability and failure in the encouragement of innovation:

> there is nothing more uncertain than the creative process and there is absolutely no innovation without failure. Show me a culture in which vulnerability is framed as a weakness and I'll show you a culture struggling to come up with fresh ideas and new perspectives.[16]

The report of the Faith and Order Commission of the Church of England into senior leadership in the Church was published as something of a counter to other papers that were forthcoming at the time, which spoke in rather hyperbolic terms about the need for success and encouragement of 'talent' in the Church[17] (more of that anon); it posed similar questions about the place of failure in leadership: 'We will certainly not encourage real improvisation and experimentation if we have generated an atmosphere of performance anxiety.'[18] Similarly, Gregory Jones and Kevin Armstrong in their book on parish ministry *Resurrecting Excellence* highlight the benefit for both leader and followers of recognizing and embracing weakness and failure: 'when we can genuinely acknowledge failure, and the vulnerability that goes with it, then we have the capacity to learn from the failure in a way that empowers both our leadership and the institution.'[19] For Jones and Armstrong, weakness coupled with strength is one of the great paradoxes (they call them 'intersections') of the Christian faith and, therefore, of successful ministry and leadership; 'For Christians, the story of the death of Jesus on the cross is a story of strength drawn from weakness, power from vulnerability, life from death.'[20]

Christians, for whom success and glory walk hand in hand with failure and death, are ideally placed to bring to leadership a healthy way of living well with the pressures and demands of our success-obsessed culture. We know that apparent failure can be the door to new opportunity and power is made perfect in weakness (2 Corinthians 12.9). We know that unless a seed falls to the ground and dies, it will not bear fruit. We know instinctively that there are different types of success and failure: apparent failure is often the pathway to success and doing things in a godly way might not always look successful to the untrained eye. That can bring great freedom to 'dare greatly',[21] to risk, to grow. A blog reflecting on the success and failures of the initial stages of a pioneer ministry reflects, for example, that 'nothing about this is comfortable, it's all risk. We didn't "succeed" in the "outcomes" of every project, but we succeeded in the way we did things, this made every project an incredible journey.'[22]

'Success' or excellence?

'Success', in ministry terms, is very difficult to define. Perhaps 'excellence' is a better concept for Christians to aim for. Paul encourages Christian disciples, 'Finally, beloved, whatever is true, whatever is honourable, whatever is just, whatever is pure, whatever is pleasing, whatever is commendable, if there is any *excellence* and if there is anything worthy of praise, think about these things' (Philippians 4.8) at the end of a long list of virtues that are to be the focus of the Christian community. Jones and Armstrong define this kind of excellence, modelled on the example of Christ in Philippians 2, as:

> an excellence that is not about our efforts or culturally defined expectations. Rather it is an excellence that is shaped by God's excellence, nurtured by new life in Christ to which we are all called in the power of the Holy Spirit.[23]

The Greek word for 'excellence' in Philippians 4 is *arete*, meaning 'virtue' or 'excellence of any kind'. It does not imply relative excellence or superiority over things, but, rather, inherent excellence in relation to the thing in question. Aristotle defines *arete* as 'a settled disposition of the mind determining the choice of actions and emotions, consisting essentially in the observance of the mean relative to us, this being determined by principle, that is, as the prudent man would determine it.'[24] The problem is that, in popular use, excellence is so often understood to mean *relative* superiority and used to rate one thing against another.

For example, the Teaching Excellence and Student Outcomes Framework (TEF) is a national exercise, introduced by the UK government to assesses teaching at universities and colleges, and to evaluate how effectively they ensure the best outcomes for their students in graduate-level employment or further study. Institutions are compared with each other in terms of the 'excellence' of their teaching, the results intended to help prospective students to decide where to study.[25] Similarly, the Research Excellence Framework (REF) benchmarks research institutions and, hence, determines where funding allocation is to be spent. Not everyone is happy about this. Research into the correlation between the supposed quality of research programmes (as determined by the REF) and the societal impact of those programmes ('change or benefit to the economy, society, culture, public policy or services, health, the environment or quality of life, beyond academia'), has shown that the link is tenuous at best. Richard Woolley and Nicolas Robinson-Garcia offer a careful critique of the way the excellence assessment is carried out, concluding that 'the very means of assessment could ultimately prove detrimental to the very thing it is seeking to encourage'. They ask, 'What if the policy's overemphasis on driving excellence leads to a homogenisation of the relationship between knowledge production and the generation of impact? Would this be beneficial, overall, for the quality, efficiency, and effectiveness of UK university research?'[26] One suspects that the answer is 'no'. Measuring excellence may be a good, or even excellent, thing to do, but we need to be careful about what it is we are measuring and what the impact of the very measurement itself may be having on those who are subject to it.

This is pertinent for the Church. There is no reason why what we do as Christians should not be at least as 'excellent' as anything that happens in so-called secular spheres. (Some churches even serve decent coffee now, so I've heard.) But we need to be wary as Christians that we do not fall into the same trap as the rest of the league-table-obsessed world and rate everything in relation to everything else in order that the Christian consumer can choose what is best. In Philippians 1, when Paul prays for the Christians in Philippi 'that your love may overflow more and more with knowledge and full insight to help you to determine what is best, so that on the day of Christ you may be pure and blameless, having produced the harvest of righteousness that comes through Jesus Christ for the glory and praise of God' (Philippians 1.9–11), the term 'best' implies godly, moral excellence, that which is different and distinctive from the way the rest of the world chooses to do things. We must be able to discern what, in God's truth, is different from the various views of measuring excellence and using those measures offered by the world around us. All our thoughts of success and excellence must be grounded in the only One who was ever excellent in any sense, either relative or absolute: Jesus Christ. Paul Tripp locates excellence in ministry in being in relationship with the person of Christ:

> Excellence in ministry flows from a heart that is in holy, reverential, life re-arranging, motivation-capturing awe of the Lord of glory. In fact, it is even deeper than that. Excellence is, in fact, a relationship. There is only one who is truly and perfectly excellent. He alone is the sum and definition of what excellence is and does. So the One who is excellence, in his grace, came to you when you were in state of anything but excellence and, by grace, offered you the promise of actually becoming a partaker of his divine nature. He then connects you to purposes and goals way higher, way grander and more glorious, than you would have ever sought for yourself.[27]

So what to do with all this? Steve Jobs once famously said, 'We are here to make a dent in the universe.' Perhaps you ask yourself, what or where, is my dent? What do we do with an inherent sense of ambition and drive for excellence, given prevailing emphases in our society (and sometimes in our Church) that laud growth and continual improvement, and yet stay in touch with the essentials of our faith and a gospel that privileges the poor and weak? How do we make a difference that counts and yet keep hold of our sanity and our soul?

It is to such things that we now turn.

2

Climbing

Dreams, indeed, are ambition;
for the very substance of the ambitious is merely the
shadow of a dream.
And I hold ambition of so airy and light a quality that it
is but a shadow's shadow.
(William Shakespeare, *Macbeth*)[1]

This is heaven to a saint: in all things to serve the Lord
Christ, and to be owned by Him as His servant, is our
soul's high ambition for eternity.
(Charles Spurgeon, *The Check Book of Faith*)[2]

Embracing godly ambition

Apparently Bristol, where I currently live, is the least ambitious city in the UK.

This despite the fact that Bristol has a great deal going for it. It is a great city with a creative and independent spirit, a developed social conscience and a hipster vibe, which is why so many of its citizens are proud to be Bristolians. But an article a few years ago in *The Spectator* suggests that Bristol is where you go to live when you've had enough of ambition:

The city has, for many years, been nicknamed 'the graveyard of ambition': a label adopted with woolly-headed pride by the locals. It's the inverted rhetoric of Bristolian exceptionalism – we're the best city on earth precisely because we don't try.[3]

Many Bristol residents, perhaps particularly those who have moved in from London and other areas of the country, would probably recognize this description of themselves. The constantly anonymous street artist Banksy (effectively Patron Saint of Bristol) famously once said, 'People who get up early in the morning, cause war, death and famine.'[4]

How are you with ambition?

I am not even sure whether Christians are supposed to have ambitions at all. Church leaders in particular aren't really supposed to be ambitious. They are not meant to have 'careers'. They have a 'vocation'. They 'discern the will of the Lord for their lives'. Church of England clergy enter, upon ordination, one of the flattest career structures in the world. The ladder lies virtually flat on the ground. Unlike many other organizations, there are no pay-scales or promotion prospects, and rightly so. You can become an area dean, or an archdeacon or a bishop, of course, but these are not supposed to be promotions. We are not supposed to speak about 'preferment'. And everyone gets the same stipend. (In theory. They don't actually, but that's another story, so don't get me started.) This is a church and not a business and Jesus had some very keen things to say about those who look for advancement and power, as we shall see.

Yet mostly it doesn't feel like that. Talk at clergy conferences and the like is often about who's in and who's out. Who will be the next to be made a bishop or archdeacon. Who is achieving 'success' in their ministry. But is that really what ambition is about? Rather than aspiration to a particular post, most clergy I know are ambitious in another sense, in that they want to do well at the 'stuff' of ministry. They want to make a difference. They want to achieve something for the kingdom of God and the good of the world. As Hill points out, 'I cannot imagine a fruitful pastor who is not ambitious, who does not dream dreams, see visions, and then work vigorously toward their realization. God is not laissez-faire, and faithful ministry is active ministry'.[5]

Is it OK to be ambitious?

I have been brought up in a culture of achievement. My parents have always encouraged me to do well. My father was a university professor and had high expectations of my own academic journey. All my life I have sought to be the very best I can be and to work as hard I can. And so I got a good set of O level results (yes, it was that long ago), was elected Head Girl, got three good A levels, went to university and just missed a first-class degree by 0.2 per cent. (The fact that I still remember that figure 30 years later tells you all you need to know.) I stayed for 11 years in higher education, stacking up the degrees as I went. I did an MPhil, a PhD (possibly just to prove to my father I could do it – a heck of a way to do that), have had a 'successful career', as far as it is possible to have such a thing as a clergy person, especially as one half of a clergy couple, have had some great opportunities and have served in some interesting places. I have sought to achieve my best in everything. I am a number 3 in the Enneagram, the Achiever, whose motto is 'I am successful.'

So a while back when I was filling in the paperwork that accompanies the process leading to senior appointment (see that's an interesting word right there: 'senior') in the Church of England, I found myself reflecting on how all this sits with my ongoing sense of achievement. A verse that has always been significant for me, ever since I was a teenager is, 'From everyone to whom much has been given, much will be required; and from one to whom much has been entrusted, even more will be demanded' (Luke 12.48). Leaving aside the fact that this verse occurs in a particularly puzzling parable where receiving a 'light beating' as a slave is apparently to be preferred over a heavy one, the challenge has always been to use the resources I have been given well and to the best of my abilities. I have been aware of having had great opportunities. I have been well nurtured and cared for, born to a relatively comfortable family with all the opportunities afforded a white, middle-class person in the affluent United Kingdom in the twenty-first century. I have had a very happy family life. I believe I have been entrusted with certain things and faithfulness requires that I steward those things wisely for the good of others. This I have done, yet the nagging thought sometimes remains, 'What if I have merely played a good game?' What if I have cleverly used my privilege and influence to strategize myself into 'senior' leadership? Have I been ambitious for 'promotion'? God is in there somewhere of course – it's all about him after all, isn't it?

Isn't it?

A while ago, I was chatting with my hairdresser and telling

him about my impending change of role, and he asked me this (to my ears) shocking question, 'So, have you always wanted to be a bishop?' At first I was completely stumped for how to answer. It's not the sort of thing I've been asked before. It's not the kind of thing you're *supposed* to ask, at least not if you move in church circles. If, God forbid, people don't understand the rules and they ask this kind of thing, as was the case with my hairdresser, the expected, Christian response is to say something like, 'No, of course not, but you know, when God calls!' (in a slightly high-pitched voice, accompanied by nervous laughter). There is a whole tradition in the Church about this, and even a Latin phrase for it, *nolo episcopari*, which is what you're meant to say in response to my hairdresser's question, and literally means, 'I do not wish to be bishop-ed'. And yet as I reflected on his question later, I realized that there are aspects of the role of a bishop that I am very much looking forward to doing and have done for some time – to be the shepherd of a whole flock, in this case a whole diocese, to have the opportunity to encourage and enable the work of God in a particular geographical area, the opportunity to support people in times of need, especially clergy and other licensed ministers, to be given permission to speak of God in the public square, to preach the gospel and to teach the word of God, guarding and passing on the faith of the apostles.

Yep. Bring it on.

Then, the day after I'd had that conversation with my hairdresser, the reading for daily prayer was 1 Timothy 3, including a verse that I had not really noticed before, 'The saying is sure: whoever aspires to the office of bishop desires a noble task' (1 Timothy 3.1).[6] The word for 'aspires' in Greek is *oregetai* and is the only place it's found in the New Testament. It means 'to stretch forward towards', and it carries a sense of desiring something inwardly, but also doing something about it, with your actions. For Paul, it was perfectly natural to desire the noble task of leadership. So, perhaps it is normal to be ambitious. It can be godly to be ambitious.

But how do we make sure that we stay on the right side of ambition?

The roots of ambition

The English word 'ambition' comes from the Latin *ambulare*, meaning 'to walk', and *ambire*, meaning 'to go around'. Its roots are found in ancient Roman politicians walking around a city canvassing for votes for election to public office. To be ambitious is simply to walk forwards. It has within it that sense of purposeful movement for the sake of upward elevation or improvement. Only later did it come to be more associated with a desire for advancement, later still with 'the object of this desire.'[7]

By the time of Shakespeare, ambition is presented as an almost universally negative attempt to rise above one's rightful place or station and in so doing offend against the laws of nature. Only the bad guys are ambitious. Or girls, if you take the case of Lady Macbeth. Mark Antony's speech after the death of Julius Caesar questions Brutus's interpretation of Caesar's actions as ambitious, in order to say something all together more positive about his dead friend:

The noble Brutus Hath told you Caesar was ambitious. /
If it were so, it was a grievous fault; / And grievously
hath Caesar answer'd it . . . / When that the poor have
cried, Caesar hath wept; / Ambition should be made of
sterner stuff.[8]

If the meaning and sense of the very word and concept of
ambition has changed over time, then we need to be aware
of its impact today, not to avoid speaking about it at all, but
to make sure that we are speaking about the right kind of
ambition and reclaiming it for what we intend to. The word
needs 'disciplining, enabling and transforming.'[9]

Ambition in the Bible

God's first command to Adam and Eve, after he had blessed
them, was, 'Be fruitful and multiply, and fill the earth and
subdue it; and have dominion over the fish of the sea and over
the birds of the air and over every living thing that moves
upon the earth' (Genesis 1.28). Having dominion over the
earth can be seen as a form of ambition, a way of doing something, of moving forward leading to improvement. The limits
of ambition in Eden are set by God himself. Humans are to
have dominion over every living thing and God provides for
them 'every tree with seed in its fruit; you shall have them
for food', but they are not to eat of the fruit of one plant, 'the
tree that is in the middle of the garden' (Genesis 3.3). Tempted
by the serpent who tells them that their ambition is only off-
limits because it will lead them to 'be like God', they go ahead
and eat.

Ever since, humans have taken what is a good and God-given gift, the gift of ambition, and used it to achieve their own desires for pre-eminence. Where ambition takes its worst form, it leads people to seek to be like God. But it doesn't have to be like this. Pioneer minister Paul Bradbury, in his book on the story of Jonah, offers an interesting take on the nature of ambition according to the two creation stories of Genesis 1 and 2, and to what he refers to as Adam I and Adam II.[10] Adam I (from Genesis 1: 'fill the earth and subdue it') represents 'the drive to create, to subdue, to use our intellect and ingenuity in the use of the materials we find around us in creation', whereas Adam II (from Genesis 2: 'work it and take care of it', alongside a desire for relationship) represents our purpose 'to serve, to surrender, to relate, to offer something of that same self in sacrifice to the wider good, the broader community.'[11] These two kinds of ambition are often in conflict with each other. Bradbury suggests that:

> We do not have to dump ambition at the threshold between one and the other; rather ambition begins to take on a more mature form, still benefiting from the drive of the charge to subdue and create, but transformed and redeemed by a deeper call to serve and offer one's gifts in the service of others.[12]

Was Jesus ambitious?

Jesus was ambitious, if by that we mean he put his all into doing the Father's will. When challenged by the Jewish leaders about his healing on the Sabbath, he answered them, 'My Father is still working, and I also am working' (John 5.17). Jesus had drive and ambition, a forward moment born of the knowledge of who he was and what he had been sent by the Father to do. However, most of the time he seemed to delight in doing exactly the opposite of the kinds of things typically taught in 'How to win friends and influence people' seminars. He wasn't very good at networking and spent time with people who were not 'strategic' and who gave him a bad reputation. After he very successfully fed 5,000 people with five loaves and two fish, the crowds were greatly impressed and said, 'This is indeed the prophet who is to come into the world' (John 6.14) and they wanted to make him King. But he didn't stay and take the adulation. Instead, he ran away up a nearby mountain. He wasn't very good at saying the right things. When he started to get some comments that his teaching was really a bit too difficult, he didn't modify his language in response to customer feedback. He said to his disciples, 'Does this offend you? Sorry – but this is the way it is.' And he lost some people from his crowd that day.

Jesus had stern words for his disciples, James and John, the sons of Zebedee, ambitious for position, when they demand of him, 'Teacher, we want you to do for us whatever we ask of you' (Mark 10.35). I would have loved to have seen the look on Jesus' face right then, but he stays calm and lets them continue. And they said to him, 'Grant us to sit, one at your right hand and one at your left, in your glory.' A very small part of me admires James and John's gall (or, if you take Matthew's account, that of their mother – acting as their agent; tiger mom at its best). But Jesus counters their request with hard talk about service and sacrifice, saying, 'whoever wishes to become great among you must be your servant, and whoever wishes to be first among you must be slave of all' (Mark 10.43–44). It seems that James and John had in mind positions of power when the Messiah entered Jerusalem, with thrones, for Jesus in the middle and they at his right and left. What they didn't seem to understand was that they were going up to Jerusalem for Jesus to die on the cross, and where on his right and left would be thieves, not thrones. Any power at work will be not military might or regal eminence, but the power of forgiveness and mercy. They truly did not know what they are asking.

Paul's ambition

Paul was a pretty ambitious person, his drive and zeal initially badly misdirected towards the persecution of Christians, until his encounter with the risen Christ on the Damascus road, and the question, 'Why are you doing this?' 'Saul, Saul, why do you persecute me'? (Acts 9.4). From that moment Paul's natural energy and ambition are pointed towards an altogether more honourable purpose, the spread of the gospel of the One whom he once persecuted, especially in places where it has not yet been heard (Romans 15.20–21).[13] As Hill puts it, 'Paul the zealous rabbi had become Paul the zealous apostle.'[14] All that mattered to Paul was to be able to say at the end of his life that he had completed what God had given him to do; 'I have fought the good fight, I have finished the race, I have kept the faith' (2 Timothy 4.7–8). His ambition was to be fulfilled not in this life but the next, when a crown of righteousness would be given to him by the only 'righteous judge'.

Perhaps precisely because Paul knew his propensity to boast, to have 'confidence in the flesh' (Philippians 3.4), he reminded others (and himself, I suspect) that the only valid reason for boasting was 'in the Lord' (1 Corinthians 1.31; see also Romans 2.23; 3.27; 4.2; 5.2, 5.11; 1 Corinthians 1.29, 1.31; 3.21; 4.7; 5.6; 9.15, 9.16; 13.3, 13.4; 15.31; 2 Corinthians 1.12). On the road to Damascus, he had the focus and object of his ambition dramatically redeemed and changed. He was still the same person with the same characteristics, but the 'telos', or end point, of his ambition was turned in the direction of Christ and his mission. When it comes to our ambitions, it is motivation that counts.

The word that we tend to translate as 'ambition' – *philotimeo-mai* (literally, 'love of honour') – is used in the New Testament in connection with three things only:

'Thus I make it my ambition to proclaim the good news, not where Christ has already been named' (Romans 15.20);

'Make it your ambition to please him' (2 Corinthians 5.9);

'Make it your ambition to lead a quiet life, to mind your own business and work with your hands' (1 Thessalonians 4.11).[15]

Paul writes to the Philippians, 'Do nothing from selfish ambition or conceit, but in humility regard others as better than yourselves' (Philippians 2.3; see also James 3.14). The Greek word translated as 'selfish, or "fleshly", ambition', *eritheia*, was associated with the concept of working for personal gain or monetary reward. It refers to seeking advancement or high office for payment. In James 3 it is listed alongside 'bitter jealousy' (see James 3.14–16) and carries the sense of striving after something someone else has, for personal benefit. It contrasts with *philotimeomai*, in that both refer to seeking office, but *philotimeomai* is with honour, rather than for monetary or personal gain. Both ambition, but two kinds, one positive and one negative. One to be pursed with honour and zeal, the other to be avoided in the Christian community.

This is not to say that, whatever our ambition, we should *not* seek to be be paid for it. After all, both Jesus and Paul affirm the Old Testament adage that 'the worker deserves to be paid' (Luke 10.7; 1 Timothy 5.18 drawing upon Leviticus 19.13; Deuteronomy 24.15). However, we do well to keep the motivation for our ambition in check when it comes to financial gain. For it to be honourable the motivation for any ambition must be about more than money. George Monbiot, writing in *The Guardian*, advocates that everyone should engage in some kind of volunteer activity, precisely *because* there is no financial reward (no possibility for *eritheia*) and any ambition you have is put to use for the good of others, or a higher cause (unless, or course, you are using your volunteering simply to enhance your own profile and look good on your CV). He says:

Perhaps it is time we saw volunteering as central to our identities and work as peripheral: something we have to do, but which no longer defines us. I would love to hear people reply, when asked what they do: "I volunteer at the food bank and run marathons. In my time off, I work for money.'[16]

Perhaps this is what Jesus was getting at when he said, 'No servant can serve two masters. Either he will hate the one and love the other, or he will be devoted to the one and despise the other. You cannot serve both God and money' (Luke 16.13, NIV). *Philotimeomai* and *eritheia* will always be adversaries.

The key to developing godly ambition is to keep an eye on our motivations. Now, as human beings, it will not always be able easily to divide the good from the sinful in terms of motivation for ambition. There is a likely to be a messy, human, muddle between the two, but my guess is that we know when we are seeking promotion in order to validate ourselves or find significance we lack elsewhere. These are the moments to check in with our motivations and our reasons for doing what we do.

So the question is what is the motivation for my ambition? Is it *philotimeomai* or *eritheia*? What am I being ambitious for? What am I aiming for? What is the end point, of my ambition?

Desire and the telos of ambition

One way to look at ambition is to see it simply as a natural form of desire or drive: 'Healthy ambition can be understood as the measured striving for achievement or distinction, and unhealthy ambition as the immoderate or disordered striving for such.' The question is what to do with that sense of drive and purpose, how to focus it, how to channel and tame it because

'Healthy ambition is life-enhancing, but unhealthy ambition is reductive and destructive and more akin to greed.'[17] A desire to accomplish something begins in childhood and has been much researched by psychologists. Robert White, for instance, posited that it is a basic human need to have an effect on one's environment through one's own efforts. He called this 'effectance motivation.'[18] Various studies have shown that ambition consists of both the mastery of a skill through effort, coupled with the affirmation essential for the motivation required for the skill to develop. Think of the child doing some action or other, while all the time shouting, 'Watch me Daddy!' We need both repeated practice *and* affirmation to encourage, tame and shape our ambitions and desires from the earliest years.

All this is not unknown to the field of Christian theology. Another common word in the New Testament closely related to this sense of ambition as an inner drive to achieve something, is what we tend to translate as 'zeal' or 'passion' (see, for example, John 2.17, 1 Corinthians 12.31, 2 Corinthians 7.7, Acts 18.25 and 1 Peter 3.13). Augustine held that God created humankind to be creatures with an innate sense of desire. That desire can either be used in the service of glory of God, or for our own ends and attempts to become more godlike. James K. A. Smith, using a broadly Augustinian perspective, describes an anthropology of human beings as creatures of desire, motivated by love, and explores the application of this framework for public life and theological education.[19] Smith claims that we are, by nature, intentional persons, 'teleological' creatures, who aim towards some end or another. We are not 'static containers of ideas or beliefs'[20] but, rather, we aim towards the world in which we live and move and have our being. He says,

'The world is the environment in which we swim, not a picture we look at as distanced observers.'[21] So, for example, it's not possible to be instructed simply to shut your and 'just think'.

Go on. Try it now . . .

What happened just then? Smith contends that you can't 'just think'. You will have been thinking *about* something. You will have, in that time, *intended towards* something. You may have been thinking, *How much longer will this chapter go on?*, or *I could do with a cup of tea* or *I don't like being told to 'just think'*. In that blank time, your desires went out towards something: the time, this page, that instruction, your need for a beverage of some kind. Furthermore, Smith goes on to suggest that we don't only *think* towards things, we *feel* towards them.[22] We have a 'gut' orientation towards the world, not primarily a head one. So in that blank time you most likely didn't *think* about time or books or tea, but you *felt* them: pages, trying to shut off thoughts, curious, tired, hot. It is more likely that you were experiencing non-cognitive reactions, not cognitive ones. Therefore, Smith says, we desire our way round the world, most markedly towards 'ultimate loves':

> that to which we are fundamentally oriented, what ultimately governs our vision of a good life, which shapes and molds our being-in-the world, in other words, what we desire above all else, the ultimate desire that shapes and positions and makes sense of our penultimate desires and actions.[23]

We are what we love and what we desire. This is what ambition looks like or, more accurately, feels like. Augustine himself was acutely aware that our desires can be either ordered in a God-ward direction or allowed to run their natural, sinful course directed by our fallen human nature. He constantly fought with his disordered desires, especially sexual ones. So it is with ambition, a 'desire for achievement'. Ambition can be either directed and 'tamed' by God, or allowed to run amok, with disastrous consequences.

We will revisit Smith's ideas further and explore their implications for those in Christian leadership in Chapter 5 when we look at what it means to desire God's kingdom more than anything else ('But strive [or desire] first for the kingdom of God and his righteousness, and all these things will be given to you as well' (Matthew 6.33)). For now we need simply to recognize that it is normal for humans, and can be godly, to be ambitious.

Perhaps all Christians should have a constant sense of unfulfilled ambition, because we have a long-term, eternal vision in which we long for the coming of God's kingdom in its entirety, which we know will not be complete until Jesus comes again and there is a new heaven and a new earth – until the Lamb that was slain has become the shepherd, until Jesus is King on earth, until there is justice for the martyrs, until every tear is wiped from every eye, there is unfinished business and you and I have a job to do. We should be in a constant state of yearning, or longing for things to be better – a sense of forward movement towards eternity. The whole of the Bible has a 'forward-facing tilt'. Ambition is part of the 'walking forward motion' with which we were created. God made us with abilities and drive, and a desire to work with him for the stewarding of all creation. He made us to be passionate about the things he is passionate about and he loves it when we put all our strategies and connections and contacts and abilities into the work of his kingdom, whether that is as a vicar, a teacher, a medic or a leader of any kind. That is what we were made for, as Ephesians 2.10 reminds us: 'For we are what he has made us, created in Christ Jesus for good works, which God prepared beforehand to be our way of life.'

Ambition and vocation

All Christians have a vocation – that is, a sense of being called forward by God to use the innate desires he has given for a purpose that glorifies him, be that as a parent, a teacher, a road sweeper, a vicar or a bishop. Sam Wells defines vocation like this:

> Vocation is a place in the soul of the believer where creation and redemption meet; that is to say, it is a place where the manner and urgency and grace with which God redeems the world in Christ through the Holy Spirit resonates with the character and disposition and qualities of the created person.[24]

Bradbury suggests that:

> Vocation is the maturing of our desires for status and purpose, the maturing of ambition. So as God seeks to nurture the desires of ambition in us, he is not wanting to stamp out such desires as though they were dirty unhealthy things. But he is deeply interested in calling

those desires into the scope of his ambitions, his love, his sovereign plans.[25]

It is not only priests and ministers who have a vocation. All Christians are called by God to use those gifts and characteristics and passions he has given them to further the work of his kingdom here on earth.

Under the umbrella of the one great vocation shared by all Christians, namely to 'Love the LORD your God with all your heart and with all your soul and with all your mind and with all your strength' and to 'Love your neighbour as yourself' (Deuteronomy 6.4–7; Mark 12.30–31; Matthew 22.37), there are a variety of subvocations. To pursue vocation is to harness that inner drive, desire and motivation to achieve something, believing these desires to have been put within us by God, and tested and affirmed by others, all of which have their own associated 'effectance motivation', requiring mastery of skills, coupled (it is hoped) with affirmation of different kinds. But if our desires are more human, fleshly, without God-ward focus, they have the potential to become destructive, for both self and those around. If the focus of ambition is purely personal gain, whether that be wealth or reputation, you are likely to lose that sense of loving what you do. There has to be a higher purpose, a higher telos. It's a matter of perspective. A Department of Education TV campaign to recruit teachers to the profession shows the immense value and lasting effect that teachers can have on the lives of their pupils. Rather than promising money, status or power, the advert holds out the more winsome, vision-focus prospect that 'Every Lesson Shapes A Life'.

The other day, someone asked me what a bishop actually does. I was very tempted to answer with some words I once heard from another bishop, 'I have no idea, but it appears to take all day.' What does a bishop do? Well, lots of meetings, oversight of safeguarding procedures, appointing new clergy, joining in with ministerial development reviews, ordaining priests and deacons, confirming candidates, preaching and teaching the faith (please, Lord!), doing media interviews, pastoral care and lots and lots of meetings, All of that stuff. Another way to answer the question is to refer to the ordinal for the consecration of a bishop, which includes words from 1 Peter. What does a bishop do?

> Shepherd the flock of God that is among you, exercising oversight, not under compulsion, but willingly, as God would have you; not for shameful gain, but eagerly; not domineering over those in your charge, but being examples to the flock. And when the chief Shepherd appears, you will receive the unfading crown of glory.
> (1 Peter 5.2–4)

That, I think, is a much better description, a much more rewarding telos for vocation to episcopacy.

So it is that whatever vocation Christians are called to follow, whatever the set of tasks each is called on to master, whatever is to be the focus of the inner desire to effect change on the world, we need that sense of higher vision and purpose described in Colossians 3.23 NIV: 'Whatever you do, work at it with all your heart, as working for the Lord, not for human masters.'

Women and ambition

Now, as I have been writing this section on ambition, a nagging thought has been bothering me. Ambition is a tricky one for women. Josephine Fairley writing in *The Telegraph* says that when ambition is 'applied to women, it's almost a slur – the subtext somehow being that ambitious women are out to trample colleagues on the ladder to success, with family and friends littered somewhere down the bottom of the life priorities list'.[26] For a start, women have a complicated relationship with power and authority. Recent high-profile books by 'successful' (why do I *always* feel the need to put that word in quotation marks?) women such as Sheryl Sandberg have encouraged a generation of women to take hold of their ambition and authority and make best use of their gifts for the good of all. And yet, especially for women raised in a more traditional Christian context, many of us have also imbibed messages about self-denial and sacrifice as ultimate virtues for all Christians, but perhaps most particularly for Christian women. For many women of my generation, we have associated godliness with meekness, owning authority with being pushy or bossy, and if someone is ambitious, it must be because they want to climb over someone else in order to achieve their goals.

It's an internal message I need constantly to monitor in myself. When I find myself in a position of authority, perhaps having a difficult conversation with a male colleague, perhaps delivering a talk at an august institution, perhaps considering taking up the office of a bishop in the Church of England, I find myself needing intentionally and deliberately to quell the internal voice that whispers that I shouldn't really be doing this, that I won't be up to it, that I will be found out, how dare I be so

ambitious? As Tish Harrison comments, 'Many of us internalize false messages about the nature of meekness, humility, and
femininity that cause us to self-sabotage and devalue our own
callings.'[27] This may be a generational thing. Observing many
of the younger female students at Trinity College it appears
that they don't always carry the same cultural and personal
baggage of my generation. Born in 1969, I am probably on the
cusp of a post-feminist generational change whereby women
younger than I were brought up with the sense that they could
do anything they put their minds to and they had no need to
prove themselves to anyone. (They may, however, be left with
other natural inclinations to overcome to do with a converse
over-obsession with self, but more of that in the chapter
that follows.) Anna Fels's research suggests that, 'There is
no evidence that the desires to acquire skills and to receive
affirmation for accomplishments are less present in women
than in men.'[28] There is no reason why, understood correctly,
and pursued for godly reasons, women should not be every
much as ambitious as men.

Developing godly ambition: some 'top tips'

1 Don't be afraid of ambition

The story of the Bible is full of people, both male and female,
who used that inner desire God had given them to step out and
take risks for him, often beyond what they saw as their own
capacity to change things. Leadership, of any shape, these days
is likely to require great courage. Perhaps we need to be a little

less squeamish about talking about ambition and the drive to get things done. The trouble is that many inherently Christian virtues such as humility, meekness, compassion and so on would appear at first glance to militate against a sense of ambition. But that is to understand ambition wrongly. As this chapter has shown, we need not to stop talking about ambition at all, but to stop talking about the *wrong* kind of ambition and to start talking about the *right* kind of ambition. When motivated by a desire to serve others, to seek the kingdom, and if it is under-girded by appropriate humility, ambition is not out of bounds for the Christian leader. Although our natural human inclination might be to seek after personal gain, and our insecurities often lead us to seek recognition, approval and glory for the wrong reasons, ambition redeemed, matured as vocation and given over to God in the service of others and of his mission can be used by him to contribute to the growth and flourishing of the kingdom.

2 Pay more attention to character

It is not wrong to aspire to senior office, in the Church or in the place of work or influence in which you find yourself. As we have seen, Paul says in 1 Timothy 3 that whoever aspires to a position of oversight 'desires a noble task'. But the verses that follow leave us in no doubt that, along with that aspiration, must come a real and sustained attention to nurturing the kind of character and living a way of life that ensures that such an aspiration never topples into 'selfish ambition'. The leader is to be 'above reproach, married only once, temperate, sensible, respectable, hospitable, an apt teacher, not a drunk-ard, not violent but gentle, not quarrelsome, and not a lover of money' (see 1 Timothy 3.3–7).

One report on leadership in the Church, rather unfortunately, stated, 'This generation of leaders faces a huge challenge in terms of *balancing* the development of their spiritual life with developing the skills needed to lead the Church through a period of profound change' (emphasis mine).[29] The thought that one needs to balance 'spiritual life' with the development of leadership skills is a profound misstep. These things are not opposites that must somehow be balanced one against the other, as if when the one lessens, the other increases. The development of the spiritual life of the leader must be completely integral to the development of the skills and competencies of leadership.

In leadership training these days there is a great temptation to want to teach only the right skills. That is understandable. Skills and aptitudes are easily practised and observed, teachable, testable, and improvements readily measurable. As long as I can teach my students *how to* counsel a person with terminal illness or *how to* prepare a sermon or *how to* develop a programme for Church growth, then all will be well, it sometimes appears. Far more difficult, yet arguably far more effective in the long run, is the development of the right kinds of character, dispositions, inclinations that will fit them for a lifetime of ministry. Smith paints a compelling picture of theological education as a shaping of the desires and imagination, the dispositions of the Christian being along these lines:

> What if education, including higher education, is not primarily about the absorption of ideas and information, but about the formation of hearts and desires? . . . What if education was primarily concerned with shaping our

hearts and passions—our visions of "the good life" – and not merely about the dissemination of data and information as inputs to our thinking? What if the primary work of education was the transforming of our imagination rather than the saturation of our intellect?[30]

Of course, in most professions and spheres of leadership developing the right skills and gaining the right knowledge is absolutely essential. If I go to the dentist, I don't care how rounded a person he is, I want him to know how to drill teeth, preferably without pain. But especially in Christian leadership the acquisition of the knowledge skills and tools for the job must go hand in hand and be deeply integrated with the formation of Christ-like character. Richard Neuhaus in his book *Freedom for Ministry* says:

It is important for seminaries to impart skills and competencies; it is more important to ignite conviction and courage to lead. The language of facilitation is cool and low risk. The language of priesthood and prophecy and the pursuit of holiness is impassioned and perilous.[31]

The more ambitious you are as a Christian leader, the more you need to pay attention to the formation of inner life, to a Christ-like character.

One question I've been asking myself recently is, what am I really doing this, or that, for? If you are someone who is ambitious – and I have already confessed to that myself – it can be tempting to see the whole of life as 'strategic', and everything we do as an opportunity to win friends and influence people.

For those of us who like to get on in life and for whom there is not much time to just sit down and have a cup of tea, the temptation to see everything we do as potentially 'strategic' is overwhelming. Strategy is a key word in the world of leadership, even in the Church, these days. You can make almost anything sound great simply by sticking the word 'strategic' in front of it. At my college we had a Strategic Plan and Strategic Goals. There are sessions on Strategic Leadership. The Church of England now hardly produces a report that doesn't have the word 'strategic' in the title somewhere. Like ambition, strategy can be good and useful, but it can also be the very thing that draws us away from our central calling to follow, not our own plans and plottings, but the call of Christ. So here's the question: Would I still do it all even if no ever knew? Would I still talk to this person if they might hinder rather than help my prospects? Will I still preach this sermon if I think it's the right thing to do even if I might lose me some friends? Would I still have that conversation even if it benefited my 'career' not one jot? Or will I only do the things that make me look good? Paying as much attention to how things are on the inside as to how things look on the outside is called integrity, and it is a vital quality in the godly leader.

The thing about Jesus is that he didn't need to prove himself to anyone. Human ambition meant nothing to him, only doing the will of his Father. Right at the start of his ministry as a dove descended, he heard those beautiful words, 'This is my Son, . . . with whom I am well pleased' (Matthew 3.17; Luke 3.22) and that carried him through everything. He heard it again at the transfiguration, at a crucial stage of his life, just before the journey to Jerusalem and the cross (Matthew 17.5;

Luke 9.35). Jesus also knew what he, and he alone, was meant to do. John's Gospel introduces Jesus' ultimate act of leadership in the upper room – washing his disciples' feet – with an interesting little phrase, easily missed:

> Jesus, *knowing* that the Father had given all things into his hands, and that he had come from God and was going to God, got up from the table, took off his outer robe, and tied a towel around himself. Then he poured water into a basin and began to wash the disciples' feet and to wipe them with the towel that was tied around him.
> (John 13.3; emphasis mine)

Jesus, *knowing* what the Father had given him to do, and where he had come from, and where he was going to, got up. Even though he was God himself, his sense of call and mission, and his inner character, prevented him from baulking at such a menial act:

> His identity, as the Son of God, didn't lead him to be arrogant and entitled, unwilling to do what needed to be done to accomplish redemption. His identity didn't cause him to assess that he was too good for the task. No, his identity motivated and propelled him to do what the disciples were convinced were below them.[32]

What would it look like for you to say that about your life and work and ministry and ambition and success? Emma, *knowing* who she was and what she was supposed to do . . . got up . . . and became the Bishop of Penrith. Sarah, *knowing* who she was in Christ Jesus, and why she had been called and who called her . . . got up . . . and served her parish as a curate. Bev, *knowing* who she was and what she was doing it all for . . . got up . . . and taught biology to year 10. Knowing who you are, whose you are and what he has given you to do requires commitment to the One in whom your identity is found first and foremost, daily self-reflection and a frequent reframing and readjusting of commitment and purpose. It starts from the inside. It is found in God.

3 Be accountable

The more ambitious you are, the more you will need others alongside you. It is not good for the ambitious leader to be alone. If we're going to change the world together, we are going to need to be each other's checks and balances to keep us in that equilibrium between authority and vulnerability. Particularly important are those deliberate relationships that have permission to comment, challenge, support and confront on life, work and ministry. Jones and Armstrong speak about the importance of 'holy friendships', those people who help us to 'overcome disordered desires, unlearn habits of sin and learn how to live faithful, holy lives in relation to God.'[33] Holy friends do three things. They 'challenge sins we have come to love, affirm gifts we are afraid to claim, and dream dreams about how we can bear witness to God's kingdom that we otherwise would not have dreamed.'[34] When it comes to keeping ambition on track with a God-ward focus, all three of these are important. Such holy friends will, if we ask them to and let them, challenge those times when ambition has slipped into *eritheia* rather than *philotimeomai*. They will help show us where our true vocation lies, including pointing out gifts, dispositions, visions and imagination that we did not even realize we had, or had been afraid to claim as our own. I clearly remember a moment when I was training for ordained ministry at theological college when my tutor, after hearing me preach on a placement, possibly only about the second time I had ever done so, told me that he thought I had a gift for communication. That early encouragement and permission to claim that gift has influenced the shape of my ministry since that day. I now try to do the same when meeting with younger leaders – spotting and speaking out words of affirmation, identifying the seeds of burgeoning gifts and dispositions. A careful and truthful word spoken, even very early on, can grow to have a much bigger effect.

To whom you are accountable?

If you don't have one already, find yourself a mentor, spiritual director, work consultant, coach, advocate, holy friend. And then, if you have someone else whose job it is to speak into your life like this, whose life are you speaking into in turn? As I step into the role of bishop, I think it's really important that I am investing in the lives of a few other leaders, particularly women, perhaps those younger than me, so that I can encourage them in the same way others have encouraged me. We have such an ideal opportunity to model leadership that doesn't pretend to have all the answers. If I can lead as me with warts and all and let others see me being me, then maybe others coming behind me might feel that they can have a go at being themselves in leadership too. Lead up and lead down. Be ambitious. But be equally ambitious for someone else.

4 Develop a keen sense of *theological* reflection

Be a theologian.

Not in the sense that you have to work in a theological college or write big books, but learn to see everything through the lens of God's word and according to the ways of his kingdom, rather than the kingdoms of this world. How do we know when our ambition is closer to godly ambition and when it is closer to selfish ambition? The answer, I believe, lies in staying close to God's word in Scripture, knowing and paying attention to the Christian tradition from which we come, keeping alert to the signs of the times, and being able to interpret each to the other, particularly noting how such things relate to our own interior landscape. In short, we need to develop and maintain an aptitude for theological reflection.

Theological reflection is something that has become very popular in the world of theological education and training for ministry in recent years. There is hardly a module at colleges up and down the country that is not assessed via a piece of work with a rubric that begins with, *Write a 2,000-word theological reflection on . . .* Indeed, even the very utterance of the phrase elects deep groans from my students. We often joke that when they leave college they will have the skills necessary to theologically reflect on a tube of toothpaste. And yet, by 'theological reflection' I simply mean the capacity to look at the world with the eyes of God.[35] Henri Nouwen in his excellent little book on Christian leadership, *In the Name of Jesus*, defines theological definition as 'reflecting on the painful and joyful realities of every day with the mind of Jesus and thereby raising human consciousness to the knowledge of God's gentle guidance'. He goes on to say, 'This is hard discipline, since God's presence is often a hidden presence that needs to be discovered. The loud boisterous noises of the world make us deaf to the soft, gentle, and loving voice of God.'[36] Nouwen insists that the task of formation for ministry should be 'deep spiritual formation of body, mind and heart in the mind of Christ'. Theological reflection is not just for trainee vicars. To be a Christian leader involves looking at your everyday work with the mind of Christ, so as allow the (often topsy-turvy) frameworks and values of the kingdom of God to direct your thinking and decision-making, rather than letting the values of any other system, be it economic or philosophical, be your guide.

This sounds much easier than it is in practice, of course, and takes a lifetime of trying, failing, getting up, being forgiven and trying again. To do this will also inevitably cause problems on occasions, especially when the values of the kingdom of God challenge, or downright contradict, the values of other kingdoms. If you are ambitious, it is likely that you'll go to a whole load of leadership conferences and read a lot of leadership books and blogs and follow many other leaders on social media. There is a great deal of wisdom to be gleaned from these sources, including sources that are not explicitly Christian, but it is important always to test everything in the crucible of the cross and resurrection of Jesus Christ.

I recently attended a leadership training course for new bishops. Before I went, I really hoped they were going to show us how to wear a mitre with style, but it turns out that wasn't what it was about at all. (Turns out that's not possible, apparently.) Anyway, at this training event, we were treated to speakers who were leaders in various organizations in healthcare, advertising and business, sharing insights from their worlds. They were excellent and I learnt a lot from what they had to say, but I was very grateful that alongside the sessions, we had times deliberately reflecting *theologically* on all that we had heard. We had a great session with a psychologist on positive thinking, but how does that resonate with the call to embrace the way of the cross on the road of suffering? We learned a lot from someone who works in advertising on how to increase 'love and respect' for your brand, but how does that sit with following a Saviour who was despised and rejected? We had a session the role of big business in transforming society, but how does that work for people who follow a Saviour who turned over the tables of the money-changers in the temple?

If we are going to aim for growth, whether in the Church or in other fields of work, and not be afraid to talk about success and embrace godly ambition, then it will be absolutely essential to also learn to think theologically about ministry and leadership, staying close to the heartbeat of Jesus, seeing everything through the lens of his kingdom, even when (especially when) it is different to the ways of the world. There is no place where this is more true than in the way we count and measure the outcomes and achievements of our work and ministry, and it is to that matter that we turn in the next chapter.

3

Counting

O My chief good,
How shall I measure out thy bloud?
How shall I count what thee befell,
    And each grief tell?
(George Herbert, 'Good Friday')[1]

Numbers are really important, but they are not the test of your holiness or your validity as a priest . . . They are important, because our job is to lead people to faith in Christ; but you look at so many stories of mission and history where people saw very little in their lifetime – but they laid roots that transformed the Church over the years.
(Justin Welby, Archbishop of Canterbury, in interview in the *Church Times*)[2]

Measuring growth and effectiveness

I have 1,042 friends.

Not actual friends, of course, but 'friends' on Facebook. Some of the people who are my closest friends are not on Facebook, and some of those 1,042 are mere acquaintances. But considering I only ever accept friend requests from people I have actually met and I never ask to 'friend' (what a word!)

students, for reasons of good boundary management, I think that's quite impressive.

I have 1,300 followers on Twitter. Oh, wait, make that 1,299 (someone just 'un-followed' me. I wonder what I did? Never mind, perhaps in a little while someone else will recognize my significance in their lives and want to follow me and receive a few daily words from me and retweets about things I consider important).

Since when has it been necessary to be able to count so accurately the number of friends or acquaintances one has? There is even a Twitter feature called 'Analytics' where one can track the impact (or 'impression') of one's Tweets, count the number of Retweets or likes, trace the numbers of followers one has gained (or lost) and compare those statistics with previous months.

(By the way, if that last sentence was gobbledygook to you and you have no idea what I am talking about – my advice? Keep it that way.)

The Vote Leave campaign ahead of the 2016 Brexit referendum was allegedly informed by data analysis companies finding out about the preferences and habits of millions of people via their social media profiles, and targeting them specifically with messages tailored to persuade them to vote to leave the European Union. Yet, having accessed this highly measurable information, it was not these potential voters' heads that were appealed to in order to win (the Remain campaign did that with numbers, facts, figures and economic predictions, labelled 'Project Fear' by the Leave camp), but their hearts, drawing on fears about immigration and what it means to be British. If the narrative of the recent TV drama, based on real events, *Brexit: The Uncivil War*[3] is to be believed, the campaign message sat relatively lightly to the accuracy of things like how much money may or may not be spent on the NHS in the event of Brexit. Algorithms were king, yet the appeal was to the primal things of the heart. Whatever your view on the rights and wrongs of Brexit, the tactics underpinning the way the referendum campaign was fought arguably highlight something of the conundrum of leadership (if we see leadership as influencing people) in the Church, in business, in education, in health care, in politics. Countables – numbers, measurements, graphs, facts and figures – drive so many policies, yet numbers never tell the full story. Hearts are rarely strangely warmed by statistics.

These days, we must analyse everything numerically. In business, education, politics, everything must be recorded, tracked, goals set and monitored. This is not necessarily a problem in itself. We need to be able to see how we are doing. It is a natural human instinct to want to assess how things are going. Humans are evaluative beings. Even the story of our creation contains a measure of . . . well, measuring. When God created the heavens and the earth, he declared it to be 'good'. 'Good' is an evaluative word. If there is 'good', there is 'worse', there is 'better' and there is 'best'. Evaluation is right there at the heart of the creation narrative, in God himself and his assessment of creation, which was good, if not better than anything.

The very first words of God to humankind are an instruction to do something: 'Be fruitful and multiply, and fill the earth and subdue it; and have dominion over the fish of the sea and over the birds of the air and over every living thing that

moves upon the earth' (Genesis 1.28). Then there is an instruction *not* to do something: 'You may freely eat of every tree of
the garden; but of the tree of the knowledge of good and evil
you shall not eat, for in the day that you eat of it you shall die'
(Genesis 2.16–17). Wherever there is a task to be done there
is the possibility of performing that task more or less well.
We know that Adam and Eve did not do so well at the second
command. They disobeyed God, choosing to forge their own
destiny by eating of the one tree they were instructed not to
touch. And so God says asks them for an account of their
actions, 'Have you eaten from the tree of which I commanded
you not to eat?' (Genesis 3.11). This is a question of assessment,
requiring them to give account of their progress (or otherwise)
towards following God's instructions, keeping his commands.
They must account for their actions.

Assessing how we are doing at things is not a bad thing
in itself. But the drive to analyse and evaluate absolutely
everything has reached epidemic proportions. In many professions there now exists a performance culture that insists
on inexorable improvement day by day, year on year. Targets,
goals, criteria, league tables, benchmarking is the language of
the workplace. Teachers lament time away from the classroom
doing what they believe they were trained to do (teaching
children) in order to fill in paperwork to do with assessment
and evaluation. A recent TV documentary about the life of
a hospital contained a poignant interview with an ear, nose
and throat consultant who decried the target-driven culture
of the NHS. His cry was that he came into the profession to
help people, not to meet targets: 'These are human beings,
not numbers.'[4] At Trinity College, during the time that I was

principal, we were inspected by UKBA, BIS, HEFCE, QAA, HESA and QiF. No, I'm not speaking in tongues – those are the acronyms of all the different groups and agencies we were accountable to as a higher education institution and a training college of the Church of England. In one sense, that's OK. Other people are giving money for us to do what we did, and my responsibility as principal was to ensure that we were doing a good job, according to a variety of measures. I can see the point of it. Sometimes things, especially in the Church, have been just a bit rubbish and we need to make sure that they're not so rubbish any more. We need to know what is going well and what is not, and to get better at it.

Even in the Church there is a drive to count everything, to quantify it, to plot it on graphs. When was the last time you went to a Church meeting that didn't have a graph in it somewhere? You can't just do something these days; you have to set goals for it beforehand, and then assess its effectiveness afterwards. The Church has got better over the years at gathering measurements and Church statistics for all sorts of different indicators, and the Church of England now has a whole department dedicated to the gathering, analysis and dissemination of statistics. This means that everyone can now see how everyone else is doing. In the diocese of which I am currently a part, colourful graphs are produced annually showing the relative stats of the different parishes, so that you (and everyone else) can see at a glance how your congregation has grown (or declined, and by how many), what your financial giving looks like, in terms of both money in the collection plate and money given by the church to the diocese central costs and so on. It also gives information about the relative socio-economic demographics of parishes and various other 'mission statistics'. The same kind of information is also available on a national level comparing dioceses. (I recently saw a similar thing ranking dioceses, using the format of the popular children's game Top Trumps, rating each according to population density, number of churches, total Sunday attendance, average weekly giving per giver and clergy headcount. But that's a whole new level of weird.)

Generally, it is good that this statistical information is clear and is freely available. And in colour! For many, its publication acts as motivation for ministry to grow and flourish. Seeing exactly how much parish A gives in relation to parish B can act as a powerful incentive to achieve greater fairness, to encourage richer parishes to support poorer ones. But for others these graphs can be a source of demotivation, discouragement and shame. It's so easy for our souls to get tangled up in the measurements. Bradbury refers to a Church beset by:

> the pressure for results, the thirst for data, the plethora of models and programmes and five year plans [which] all speak of an organisation whose trust in the call of God on those who are working out their vocation as ministers in the church is increasingly tempered by anxious managerialism.[5]

And yet we need to measure things. We need to know where we are in order to know what to do next and to know how to steward our resources well. One of the skills of the good leader is to 'know how to help people confront reality in a way that honestly faces the important issues and at the same time preserves their self-esteem.'[6] Part of this reality is bound to include numbers.

How do we count and what should we count?

In 1963 sociologist William Bruce Cameron, in a book on measuring in the field of sociology, wrote:

> It would be nice if all of the data which sociologists require could be enumerated because then we could run them through IBM machines and draw charts as the economists do. However, *not everything that can be counted counts, and not everything that counts can be counted.* (emphasis mine)[7]

The way we count, and what we count or measure, demonstrates what we consider to be important; 'To measure is to shape the culture with a microcosm of your leadership worldview.'[8] What values are we encouraging or promoting through our measurements? For instance, Archbishop of Canterbury Justin Welby's 2017 Lent book *Dethroning Mammon* laments that fact that we often too readily focus on things that can be easily counted, such as GDP (gross domestic product), while neglecting other, highly valuable but less easily quantifiable 'goods' such as voluntary labour.[9] So as Christian leaders, choosing what to measure and count will give an indication about what we hold to be important. No measurement is devoid of value because 'all numbers are designed by people and interpreted by people'.[10] We might paraphrase as, 'Where your graphs are, there your heart is also.'

In Church of England terms, the number of people going to church each Sunday, as well as the number attending the major festivals and the numbers of baptisms, weddings and funerals, has been declining.[11] The percentage of people in the UK calling themselves 'Christian' shows a downward trend too. The reasons for this are too varied and complex to unpack here. What I will say, however, is that there is now a renewed effort to do something about it. And that begins with counting it.

For Church leaders, in the Church of England at least, the most common measures are 'average weekly attendance' or 'usual Sunday attendance', which are ascertained by asking local churches to survey their congregations (usually in October) and send the information in to Church House, from which the Statistics Unit produces a very informative report and some pretty graphs. That is also the figure sent for the diocese to produce its colourful charts, and that is the figure which is quoted on job adverts for the vicar's post (but usually only if it's high enough to be thought of as a potential draw).

However, patterns of living and, hence, church attendance are changing. Many families now find themselves engaged in other activities on a Sunday morning, attending sports clubs and so on. Additionally, other kinds of worship events have become more popular, like midweek services such as Messy Church. In addition, the way people belong to the Church is changing. Along with the decline in membership of other institutions, such as political parties and unions, comes a decline in people considering themselves 'signed up members' of churches (even of churches such as the Church of England that don't have official membership). People now are more likely to be nervous of jumping in with both feet and would prefer to hover around the edges before committing. Many church leaders now speak of an 'active fringe' rather than a 'committed central core'. People come to church less often. Events such as men's groups, curry evenings and 'Hymns we love' lunches have become more popular, possibly because they allow people to engage with the community of the church and the things they see on offer there without committing to regular church attendance. But how to measure such things? It gets even more challenging when we need to work out how to assess less tangible or observable measures, such as growth in discipleship.

A renewed emphasis on numerical church growth is good, important and necessary. I am not going to decry the need for churches to grow, and to grow numerically. As David Goodhew points out, there is strong theological justification for the growth of the Church:

> The Christian faith holds that the good news of Jesus, whilst it has to be received as an individual, can be received only in a community. So, growing such communities multiplies such blessing. To keep the good news to oneself would be both mistaken and selfish . . . God loves individual human beings and God loves Christian congregations. So the numerical growing of congregations is a godly and essential means of mediating that love.[12]

We do need to focus on growth in numbers. We need to rejoice as men and women and children come into God's kingdom – one by one by one. As Ian Paul states in a blog post on church attendance statistics, 'measuring these numbers is important, because numbers are people, and if people matter then numbers matter,' but he also says, 'we need to be clear what we are measuring, and ensure that we measure what we value rather than simply valuing what we measure'.[13] There may be mixed motives behind measuring church growth. Some reasons for wanting the Church to grow are excellent (more people coming into the kingdom of God); some efforts towards church growth are thinly veiled power trips by self-obsessed leaders.

So, what good reasons might there be for counting and measuring, and what kinds of motivation are less healthy and do we need to recognize and avoid? How do we stay on the right side of the counting and see measurements and statistics as friendly and helpful rather than threatening and embarrassing?

Four good reasons for counting and measuring things

1 The Bible plays the numbers game

Numbers are important in the Bible. There's even a book called . . . Numbers. In fact, you might say that the biblical writers seem fairly obsessed with numbers: six days of creation (and one rest day), 12 tribes, animals in pairs, 12 disciples, the feeding of the 5,000, groups of 50, 12 baskets, 3,000 converted in Acts 2, 5,000 in Acts 4, 144,000 sealed in Revelation. Again and again, things and people are counted for a variety of reasons, some of them bad, some of them good.

The Hebrew verb *mdd* (to measure) occurs 52 times in the Old Testament, and there is a great range in what is measured. One of the ways God's almighty power is shown is in the fact that he measures, weighs and assesses things of the earth. For example. 'He stood, and measured the earth: he beheld, and drove asunder the nations; and the everlasting mountains were scattered' (Habakkuk 3.6).[14]

God alone is the one who can measure the earth and its inhabitants correctly in order to judge them, and thus is his sovereignty demonstrated, 'Who has measured the waters in the hollow of his hand and marked off the heavens with a span, enclosed the dust of the earth in a measure, and weighed the mountains in scales and the hills in a balance?' (Isaiah 40.12). God's questioning of Job about his nature and deeds includes the challenge, 'Where were you when I laid the foundation of the earth? Tell me, if you have understanding. Who determined its measurements – surely you know!' (Job 38.4–7). Counting shows the power of the judgement of an almighty God. Additionally, God's people are to emulate him in fair and accurate assessment, measuring and counting things honestly and correctly.

One of the marks of God's people was that they measured things well: 'You shall not cheat in measuring length, weight, or quantity. You shall have honest balances, honest weights, an honest ephah, and an honest hin. I am the LORD your God, who brought you out of the land of Egypt' (Leviticus 19.35–36). In weighing correctly they identify themselves as God's people, and reflect the nature of the one who likewise shows no dishonesty or prejudice in measuring. Indeed, the ability to weigh and measure things correctly is linked to God's blessing that, if you weigh and measure things honestly, God will let you enjoy a long life in the land he's giving you (Deuteronomy 25.15). Several times in Proverbs the importance of honesty in measuring is highlighted: 'false balance is an abomination to the LORD, but an accurate weight is his delight' (Proverbs 11.1); 'Diverse weights and diverse measures are both alike an abomination to the LORD' (Proverbs 20.10; see also Proverbs 20.23; 16.11).

The reason for God's displeasure with false measurement is his concern for the poor and oppressed, who are the ones who most lose out in any dishonest system. One (of many) of the complaints the prophet Amos has against the people is that they 'trample on the needy, and bring to ruin the poor of the land' because they 'practise deceit with false balances, buying the poor for silver and the needy for a pair of sandals, and selling the sweepings of the wheat' (Amos 8.4–6).

The New Testament writers seem equally to be concerned to record numbers where they add to the meaning of the message being conveyed. John, for example, is at pains to tell us that at the wedding of Cana there were 'six stone water-jars for the Jewish rites of purification, each holding twenty or thirty gallons' (John 2.6). He wants us to be in no doubt that this is a lot of wine we're talking about here. However, Jesus does funny things with numbers, and his teaching exposes a kingdom economics that is very different from the economics of this world. When Jesus overturned the tables of the moneylenders in the temple he was violently protesting against an economic, religious and political system that exploited the outsider and valued some people more than others, exploiting the lowest for financial gain. And so, for Jesus, the widow's smallest mite was the best, the first shall be last, those who show up to work late get paid the same as those who arrive early, when you feed people with faith five loaves and two fish is enough, and there is more left over. The sums are subverted, the chains of supply and demand are broken, and the oppressed go buy-one-get-one-free.

Although the Gospel writers are keen to record that 'large crowds' followed Jesus to hear his teaching, Jesus himself simultaneously points out the radical hospitality of the gospel (the parable of the Banquet), while also pointing out the cost of following him, which must be calculated and considered by would-be disciples: 'Whoever does not carry the cross and follow me cannot be my disciple. For which of you, intending to build a tower, does not first sit down and estimate the cost, to see whether he has enough to complete it?' (Luke 14.27–28).

The story of the growth of the Church in Acts scrupulously records a detailed accounting for those whom 'the Lord added to their number' (Acts 2.47): 3,000 new followers of Jesus in Acts 2.41, 5,000 in Acts 4.4, 'great numbers' in Acts 5.14 and 'a great many priests' in Acts 6.7.

Yes, the Bible does numbers pretty well, which is why it must surely be significant, and rather sobering, that at the end of time, standing before the throne of the Lamb, will be a great crowd, 'that no one could count, from every nation, from all tribes and peoples and languages' (Revelation 7.9). The end of counting. Counting is a provisional, earthly need necessary to govern and fill and subdue the earth while we have other fallible human kings and rulers. Once God is King, and the kingdom of God comes in full on this Earth, we shall have no need to count at all, for all will be gathered in.

2 There is growth in the kingdom of God

When Jesus burst on the scene proclaiming 'The time is fulfilled, and the kingdom of God has come near; repent' (Mark 1.15), he was building on the long-held belief that God would one day bring his rule and reign to the world. The Old Testament prophets looked forward to the time when God's Messiah would come and 'The LORD will become king over all the earth' (Zechariah 14.9). Jesus came to inaugurate that kingdom, the power of the rule of God breaking increasingly into the present, which won't be complete until the end of time when God's rule is fully established on earth. The kingdom of God is arguably the central tenet of Jesus' teaching, which is why he used so many different images and pictures and stories to describe and explain it – and why people quite often didn't get what he was on about (see Mark 4.11, 4.9; Matthew 13.13; Luke 8.10). It is striking how many those pictures describe the kingdom of God in terms of natural things that grow – seeds, trees, yeast. It is an imagery continued by Paul in such as 1 Corinthians 3.6: 'I planted, Apollos watered, but God gave the growth.' Although we must not make the mistake of thinking of the kingdom as coterminous with the Church (the kingdom is much wider than the Church, having an eschatological horizon), and we must not confuse kingdom growth with Church growth (still less Church 'success'), nevertheless it remains the case that there is something about God's kingdom that presupposes growth, movement, vitality, even expansion. As McGrath puts it, 'The characteristic images of the kingdom – yeast spreading in dough, seeds growing in the ground – indicate that some kind of growth is integral to the New Testament vision of the gospel.'[15]

There seems to be somewhat of a trend around at the moment to assert that when it comes to the things of God, small is better. Possibly reacting against an overemphasis on Church growth and the exultation of larger churches in recent years, the penchant among some influential Christian thinkers now is rather to laud all things small, insignificant, unimpressive. Shane Claiborne, for instance, says, 'We worship the seed that died. . . . Get ready, friends, God is preparing us for something really, really – small.'[16] What Claiborne is referring to is the work of Christian mission existing in local, unspectacular ways, showing small acts of kindness and community hope. This is, of course, to be welcomed and encouraged. Small can indeed be beautiful (think of faith the size of a mustard seed) but to deliberately *aim* for the Church to be small is to miss the point. Churches can be small, of course, in which case there should be lots of them.

We know that growth is not to be understood *only* in terms of numbers. Stephen Spencer draws on Avery Dulles' models of the Church in painting a picture of growth in the Church that exists on two planes – that of gathering and dispersal. Growth, correspondingly, occurs in both directions of movement:

it cannot be just about an increase in the size of the gathered church viewed as a self-contained institution. This would be to distort the nature of the church. Instead, both directions of movement must be taken into account: church growth needs to be seen as an increase in the reach and scope of that movement, in the extent of both gathering and dispersing.[17]

The growth must be in both in numbers and in effect, influence, interaction with local communities, as well as the discipleship of Christians.

Theologically speaking, when we take note of fact that God sent his Son into the world so that the world would come to know him, and that the Son sends his disciples to 'go into all nations, baptising and teaching', the implication is that the knowledge of God and the growth of his kingdom is supposed to spread, and become – numerically – bigger. As Goodhew points out:

> the numerical growth of congregations [is] heartily to be desired. Local congregations . . . are beloved by God. Who are we to devalue that which God values so highly? Since congregations are so highly valued by God, their growth and proliferation is at the heart of the kingdom and at the heart of the Christian mission.[18]

So I am not with those who extol small churches as something to deliberately aim for. There may be all kinds of reasons why the church is small (for instance, persecution or low population in an area), and small churches can be excellent at discipleship and mission and all the things churches are supposed to be, but the fact remains that part of our job as Christians is to help them not to remain small, as far as possible, through the preaching of the beautiful gospel of Christ and the winning of souls for the kingdom. Small might indeed be beautiful, but then if the small thing *is*, in fact, beautiful, why would more and more people not want to come and join the small, beautiful thing? Why not lots and lots of beautiful, small things all over the place? In other words small (or big) are not virtues in themselves when it comes to church size. What is good, is individual people coming to know Jesus Christ and becoming part of his body on earth.

Does size matter? Yes, it does.

3 Numbers matter because people matter

In 2 Samuel 24 (also in 1 Chronicles 21), King David tells his army commander Joab to count all his soldiers (in 2 Samuel it is at the incitement of God himself, and in 1 Chronicles at the incitement of Satan). Joab says back to him, 'May the LORD your God increase the number of the people a hundredfold, while the eyes of my lord the king can still see it! But why does my lord the king want to do this?' (2 Samuel 24.3), questioning whether the counting is really such a good idea. But the counting happens, and afterwards David is filled with remorse for doing so, 'I have sinned greatly in what I have done' (2 Samuel 24.10). This is not because counting is wrong, but because David has been prompted by pride and selfish ambition, and a failure to trust in God.

Counting people is a dangerous activity, it seems. The Old Testament writers seemed to be acutely aware of the perils of counting wrongly, probably because they were aware of the fact that to 'reduce' (note the language) someone to a mere number was to devalue their unique personhood: 'Counting always carries the risk that it 'devalues the individual and tends to make him or her replaceable.'[19]

In Exodus 30, when God commands Moses to take a census of the people, he also warns him, 'When you take a census of the Israelites to register them, at registration all of them shall give a ransom for their lives to the LORD, so that no plague may come upon them for being registered' (Exodus 30.11). In a context where the more people you had, the more economic and military might you had, God wanted his people to be different, and to recognize that:

> the human person as such, man or woman, rich or poor, powerful or powerless, is the image of God and therefore of non-negotiable, unquantifiable value. We are each equally in the image of God, therefore we stand equal in the presence of God.[20]

Counting can be either valuing or devaluing of people. It is most dangerous when it masks or denies the humanity or value of real people. Rabbi Jonathan Sacks says that 'The numbering of a people is the most potent symbol of mankind-in-the-mass, of a society in which the individual is not valued in and for him- or herself but as part of a totality whose power lies in numbers.'[21]

But counting can also be caring, rather than sinister. One of the ways the Psalmist describes how much God values us is that he knows the number of hairs on our heads. Jesus' parables are full of people counting things, so that they know what was missing or lost – coins, pearls, sheep, sons. Ninety-nine sheep are left in favour of the search for the one. God cares about numbers because God cares about people. The Jewish commentator Rashi asserts that when God counted his people in the Torah, it is because he loves them. In a comment on the census recorded in Numbers 1, he says:

Because they are dear to Him, God counts them often. He counted them when they were about to leave Egypt. He counted them after the golden calf to establish how many were left. And now that He was about to cause His presence to rest on them, he counted them again.[22]

The Hebrew word for 'count' in this passage has the meaning 'to lift the head', *se'u et rosh*, conveying 'insistence on the the dignity and integrity of the individual'.[23] To lift someone's head is to really see them, to know them. It is 'a gesture of love'.[24]

For the Jewish people, counting has carried with it a particular significance, especially in relation to the darkest period of their history. At a visit to Yad Vashem, the World Holocaust Memorial Centre in Jerusalem, a couple of years ago, I was struck by the powerful combination of an insistence on engaging meticulously with the numbers – which are staggering and awful – coupled with the careful remembering and telling of the stories of individuals, with names, faces, individual lives and deaths. The Hall of Names seeks to tell the story of each named victim. Another room lists the approximate numbers of Jewish people killed in each European country, about 6 million in total.[25] The counting and plotting of the statistical effects of the Holocaust, which are still ongoing, is coupled with a tireless and moving work to name and document the testimony of each and every one of those individuals. Both approaches are still very much needed. A poll carried out by Opinion Matters for the Holocaust Memorial Day Trust in 2019, shockingly, revealed that one in 20 people do not believe the Holocaust ever took place.[26] And 64 per cent of people polled did not know how many Jews were murdered or grossly underestimated the number. If we kept a moment's silence for every victim of the Holocaust, we would be silent for 11 and a half years. These kinds of numbers matter because they, in themselves, tell a story.

Numbers are important. Counting things is necessary. It shows us the scale of things: things we wish to celebrate, and things we need to lament, repent of and remember. But individual persons and their names are equally, if not more, important. When we measure and count things, both are necessary.

4 Counting helps us to know where we are

One of the tasks of Christian leadership is to enable the good stewarding of resources. Jesus told the parable of the Talents to show that in his kingdom, careful and faithful management of the resources (not only financial, but also time, energy, gifts and so on) is expected by the 'Master' (see Matthew 25.14–30, Luke 19.11–27).

We need to know where we are (and where we have been) in order to know where we're going. Max De Pree famously said, 'The first responsibility of a leader is to define reality. The last is to say thank you. In between the two, the leader must become a servant and a debtor. That sums up the progress of an artful leader.'[27] Defining reality inevitably involves getting to grips with the numbers. Valler includes understanding the power and significance of measurement as one of the key tools for effective leadership: 'Good leaders understand the role of measurement in pursuing purpose and are sensitive to its motivational, relational and cultural impact.'[28] Indeed, Gil Rendle in his book, *Doing the Math of Mission*, claims that an ability to measure things well is 'now at the leading edge of wilderness skills that church leaders need to learn in our journey into a changed mission field'.[29] Being able to draw an honest picture of current reality, with clarity, is an immensely important factor in helping any organization to move forward. That includes the metrics, financial reality, achievement figures, sales figures, GCSE results, operating results and so on.

When I took up my post as principal of Trinity College, the number of students was at a rather low ebb. Following some years of high recruitment, for various reasons the graphs had started to go in the wrong direction. Each student, whether Church of England ordinand or student funding his or her own study by another means, brings in a certain amount of fee income to the college. There are no outside sources of funding, so low student numbers meant that the college was potentially in a precarious position.

Now, I was not attracted to the role of principal of a theological college because I am an accountant or a businesswoman or because I particularly relished running an organization. I am a community-builder, a communicator, a theologian, someone who cares about learning and discipleship, churches, people and the mission of Jesus Christ. However, on taking up my post, it was clear that one of the things which needed to be done quickly was to increase student recruitment. There needed be an honest assessment of numbers, some analysis of why this might be the case, then numbers needed to increase. Therefore, 'To increase and sustain student recruitment' was set as a 'key strategic goal' for the next five years. It was communicated as such among all the college staff. Systems and approaches were created and changed in order to enable it. Seemingly small operational decisions were affected by a focus on the goal. For instance, the decision was made to locate the admissions officer in the same office as the communications manager, in the knowledge that if those two key roles understood each other's perspectives and were able to communicate regularly and effectively, recruitment was more likely to rise.

Thankfully, by God's grace, student numbers rose dramatically; numbers of students studying for ordained ministry doubled in four years. The focus on increasing student numbers was not because I care more about the figures than the people. It was precisely because I care about people and their ministry in the Church that the numbers had to be carefully managed and monitored, because without healthy numbers of students, there would be no college, and with no college, there would be none of the education, formation and training that we believed God had called us to do. It is the role of the leaders of an organization, a college, a church, to be aware of the numbers and statistics, to interpret their meaning and to communicate their significance to colleagues, while keeping before them always the priority of people and not allowing the numbers to depress or demotivate.

So there are some very good reasons for counting things. But just keep an eye on your soul, won't you? This is a book about leadership, and my concern is what an emphasis on counting and measuring, whether Church growth or any other metric used in your sphere of work or ministry, which might well be good, timely and theologically justified, can do to leaders, if understood and approached wrongly.

Four bad reasons for counting and measuring things

1 Because we imagine that if we count things, they will automatically grow

Counting things doesn't necessarily help things to grow. It is quite possible to be acutely aware of the metrics and statistics of your organization and to be simultaneously doing precious little about it. One of my favourite phrases is this: 'Weighing the pig doesn't fatten it.' In terms of weighing the pig of Church growth, I sometimes wonder if we have even agreed what we're supposed to be feeding it in the first place.

First of all, we need to note that counting and measuring are not the same thing. Rendle explains that counting involves giving attention to numbers, and answers the questions: How many? How often? How much? Measuring, however, pays attention to change, addressing the question, How far?[30] It is important, he says, to pay attention to such things as resources and activities, which can be measured, as well as to the 'vitality' of a congregation, which is 'a measure of the potential of the congregation for accomplishing the real outcome of ministry, which is making disciples and changing the world.'[31] When God created Adam and Eve, he told them to both be fruitful (a measuring thing) and to multiply (a counting thing), to fill the earth (a counting thing) and subdue it (a measuring thing).

Both measuring and counting are important. But even they don't describe the whole picture. When we focus too much on counting and measuring resources and activities at the expense of describing hoped-for outcomes (how far and in what time?) we become fixated on scarcity, which can lead to fear and anxiety; 'While we need to know many things about our churches that can be counted, we are limited when we over-focus on things simply because we know how to count them.'[32]

It is not only about what we can observe now, it is also about what we would like to see in the future – and that relates to intended outcomes. Outcomes, which are about purpose, goals and discernment, and involve a certain degree of dreaming, can be better described than measured: 'The outcomes we need are those deep, even disturbingly clear, descriptions of what we believe can be different if God gets involved . . . this is no longer problem solving, it is possibility hunting.'[33]

Rendle holds together the necessity of analysing and assessing the metrics with the fact that counting anything will never sufficiently capture the essence of what ministry in the Church is about:

> Ministry is, more importantly, about some change in a person, a congregation or a community because of the presence of Christ. Such change is the *why* of ministry, and the why does not lend itself so easily to numbers as does the present *what* of the congregation.[34]

The same could possibly be true of the *why* of teaching, for instance, or social care. Although counting might be necessary in all of these fields, no one ever went into teaching because they were passionate about tracking the school's league table positioning, but because they wanted to make a difference in the lives of young people.

Counting things won't make them grow. In itself, counting and measuring improves nothing. But using measurement and describing outcomes effectively may help a community more accurately assess the realities, which may in turn help it to move more effectively and realistically towards the vision-filled changes it wishes to see.

2 Because we imagine that having targets will make things work better

Targets are certainly the order of the day in health care and education, and in some business sectors. The setting of targets was a key tenet in the ethos of the New Labour government of the 1990s, where 'targets were linked to dedicated budgets allocated by the Treasury.'[35] And yet it appears that targets do not necessarily provide an effective incentive for achievement, and can in fact mean that the more subtle aspects of policy change are overlooked in favour of quick and easy measurements.

In the arena of climate change science, an article in *The Guardian* alleges that a culture of 'targetism' is hindering, rather than helping, the reversal of climate change as well as the development of effective policies to do so, because:

a linear translation of scientific evidence into managerial targets is an ineffective way of using evidence in policy. Rather than the messy balancing of economic, environmental and social goals for sustainability, climate policy provided a logic of turning to science for numbers which could be transplanted into managerial targets.[36]

Likewise, as an interview with surgeon David Grant shows, targets can be liable to provide a false sense of success, especially when the setting of those target levels is somewhat arbitrary. Grant, commenting on an 85 per cent target for patients starting treatment within 62 days of referral, says:

> That's great and it's noble and it's wonderful . . . but what about the other 15 per cent? They are still people. Is it OK for them to not get treated in 62 days? To me the target should be 100 per cent.[37]

So it turns out that setting targets is not the best way to determine policy, or to effect change. Not many churches have growth targets, but some church-based projects, especially those that attract grant funding, have what are termed 'expected outcomes' – a certain expected level of growth or increase within a period of time. The problem is that having a target, or expected outcome, can both be motivating, something to aim for, but also become all-consuming or threatening when it looks as if it might not be met. Church work and ministry in particular is messy and unpredictable, and there may be all sorts of reasons why targets are not achieved or not in the expected timescale. The effect on the morale of the leaders involved in this case is not to be taken lightly.

3 Because numbers validate our existence

On a good day as principal of Trinity, I was concerned with the numbers because I wanted to see more and more people benefiting from the excellent kingdom-focused training for ministry our college offered. On a bad day my focus on the numbers arose more out of a concern for my own reputation and a desire to be seen as successful, especially as the only female college principal at that time.

It is possible for leaders to become infected with a rather nasty disease called 'numeritis'. (That's a made-up word, by the way, before you look it up in the dictionary.) Numeritis is a condition whereby you become obsessed with numbers. I've seen it happen in others and I have seen it in myself. So how do you know if you've got it? The symptoms are varied but can include the following: when there has been a church event you weren't at, before asking how it went, you ask how many people were there; when telling people about your numbers – how many in your church, what your giving figures are like and so on – you round them up by about 10 per cent to make them sound just a little bit better; when you begin to suspect your moods are affected by the latest data more than you care to admit; or when you begin to use phases like 'according to the dials on my dashboard, that is a highly effective ministry'; and, not even ironically, when you constantly look over your shoulder to see what others' numbers are like in comparison with yours.

The trouble is that one of our major world leaders at the moment has a rather bad case of numeritis. President of the USA Donald Trump became very upset when photographs revealed that many more people had attended his predecessor's inauguration than his. When faced with the lowest electoral vote ever, Trump claimed it was because three to five million people (always good to be precise about these things) who had voted for his opponent, Hilary Clinton were, in fact, ineligible voters. Trump has a bad case of numeritis. You and I aren't like that, are we? Actually, I could tell you exactly how many students in several different categories Trinity admitted each year I was principal. And exactly how the June figures tracked with those at the same point in the previous year. And I could probably give you some comparable stats for other theological colleges in the country too. So – numeritis? Hmmm.

4 Because we're anxious and afraid

An obsession with counting things can betray an unholy lack of confidence in the call and equipping of Christ in our lives, and, in the case of church growth, his promise that he will build his Church and the gates of hell will not prevail against it. Conversely, we are determined that this ship shouldn't go down on our watch. Bonhoeffer pointed out that there is no inevitable link between apparent growth and the health or otherwise of the Church, and that leaders should not be anxious:

> It is not we who build. He wills to build the church. No man builds the church but Christ alone. Whoever is minded to build the church is surely well on the way to destroying it; for he will build a temple to idols without wishing or knowing it. We must confess – he builds. We must proclaim – he builds. We must pray to him – he builds. We do not know his plan. We cannot see whether he is building or pulling down. It may be that the times which by human standards are times of collapse are for him the great times of building. It may be that the times

which from a human point of view are great times for the church are times when it is pulled down. It is a great comfort which Christ gives to his church; you confess, preach, bear witness to me, and I alone will build where it pleases me.[38]

That's all very well, and whereas the success or otherwise of the Church may be hidden to all but God, most of what we count is made very public. School league tables are published, church growth statistics are posted on church websites for all to see, the relative numbers of the various theological education institutions are shared with the General Synod of the Church of England and anyone else who cares to look, and the relative ranking of hospitals is emblazoned on the front pages of the national newspapers. For some leaders, this might be motivational, especially for those whose graphs are going in the right direction. For others it can be the source of deep shame and anxiety, especially for leaders who, for whatever reason, are not seeing the growth they would like to. Martyn Percy worries that in the Church, 'Sharp missional evangelistic thinking has created a culture where clergy feel like employees, chasing targets – and they feel guilty when they don't achieve those targets, or when they can no longer relate to what has become an organisation.'[39] The temptation to achieve significance through numbers can potentially cause leaders to seek to control others in order to achieve the ends they seek. Eugene Peterson points out this danger that:

Under the pressure of 'working for Jesus' or 'carrying out the church's mission' we begin to treat our family members and fellow workers more like part of a machine than parts of a body. We develop a vocabulary that treats men and women and children more like problems to be fixed or as resources to be used than as participants in a holy mystery. . . . assets and liabilities, point man or woman, dysfunctional, leadership material, dead weight. Love, the commanded relation, gives way to considerations of efficiency interpreted by abstractions – plays and programmes, goals and visions, evangelism statistics and mission strategies.[40]

It is so easy to become anxious in the face of apparent decline. Of course, Christ has no hands and feet on earth now except ours, and the responsibility and honour of working to bring increase in the kingdom of God and the common good of the world around us sits on our shoulders. But it is a burden we do not carry alone. Perhaps the need, above all, is to return to the God who called us in the first place, to set all of our efforts and endeavours in the context of the larger picture of God and his plan, to begin to think theologically about mission, ministry, work, counting and measuring.

Counting theologically

It is the contention of this book that the Church is supposed to grow, in depth, commitment, numbers and any other which way that can be named and thought of. But it also true that we must look at such growth with the eyes of God, through the lens of theology, otherwise it will be all too easy to be carried away by theories and motivations for growth that belong to another kingdom and to other gods, more to do with power, wealth and dominance than with the cross and resurrection of Christ. Alister McGrath holds that theology is essential for thinking well about Church growth:

> Theology matters to church growth, precisely because it aims to sustain the luminous and captivating vision of God which lies at the heart of the Christian faith, defending it against well-meaning attempts to reduce it to something manageable and culturally accessible, which ultimately robs it of its depth and vitality.[41]

Two key Christian themes or doctrines in particular make counting and measuring different for Christians, and especially for Christian leaders, compared with people who do not have a Christian world view in mind.

The first is eschatology. In order to measure something effectively, it is generally assumed that this will involve a certain timescale. To know whether something has been done or not, and therefore to be able to measure or count it, there needs to be an end date or time by which it was supposed to be completed. To measure growth, one needs to do that over time. To assess whether something has hit a target, there needs to be a point in time at which that target is located. But the trouble is that God has no beginning and no end. God's people are part of a story that began before creation ('since before the foundation of the world' [Ephesians 1.4]) and which will not end ('there will be no more night; they need no light of lamp or sun, for the Lord God will be their light, and they will reign for ever and ever' [Revelation 22.5]). Ever. One day our work on earth as we know it will be done, but Jesus was insistent that we do not know when that day will be, 'about that day and hour no one knows, neither the angels of heaven, nor the Son, but only the Father' (Matthew 24.36). Perhaps that is to stop us trying to measure things too much.

So all this means that the work of God in the world is never finished. It therefore follows that all measurements need to have about them a measure of provisionality; the end is *not* in sight. And yet in another sense the end, as in the end of our time on this earth, is *always* in sight, with the eyes of faith. We always have a view that is higher and further and deeper than anything we can actually see because we believe in life after death, and a kingdom that will have no end. As McGrath puts it:

> An eschatological perspective challenges the privileging of the present, forcing us to take the long view – thinking in terms of centuries, not years. None of us sees the 'big picture', which allows us to grasp the significance of our present in the greater scheme of things.[42]

As a college principal there was a great pressure upon me to prepare people for the 'Church of the future' (as if it were ever possible to guess what that might look like). It is all too easy to look at the present challenges facing the Church, and theological education, which are many, and to attempt to 'future-proof' it all. I understand this pressure, and it is certainly preferable to training ministers for a Church that has long disappeared into the past. But there can be a certain tyranny in trying accurately to second-guess, and position for, the future. Rather, the task of theological education is to prepare the kinds of people who instinctively desire the things of God's kingdom. Because we don't know exactly what the future will be like, we need leaders who are able to think theologically in line with kingdom values and so are prepared to face any question and any circumstance. We will explore further what it means to lead in a manner that honours an eschatological perspective in Chapter 5, when we look at leading in the power of the Holy Spirit. Although it might be important to measure and predict all kinds of things, a Christian leader will inevitably have a sense of vision and timescale that transcends and supersedes anything that might be gleaned from the here and now alone. To have faith means:

> embracing and inhabiting this greater story and recalibrating and redirecting own own stories in its light. We find proper meaning and value through being part of this grand narrative, which transcends our individual narratives yet gives them new significance and signification.[43]

The second theological theme that ought to inform our counting and measuring is the doctrine of grace. Valler states that:

> measuring well involves navigating through the tension between performance and grace. Performance does matter, but at the deepest level it does not affect the value of people. The art of measurement is to bring truth, learning and accountability without leaving people feeling judged, threatened or devalued, to bring focus and motivation without making people feel driven.[44]

Most measurements are about assessing how well something has been done, and whether certain standards have been met. At the heart of the Christian faith is the countercultural claim that we cannot save ourselves, but only God can, that no amount of effort will lead to greater salvation, which is sheer gift, and that life in Christ cannot be worked for (still less measured), but only received.

Measuring is often to do with performance, assessment and relative effectiveness, all of which concepts are anathema to grace. Jesus Christ was the only one who ever 'performed' anything 'effective' in terms of eternal salvation, and Christians are assessed purely on the basis of his 'efforts' (the quotation marks come thick and fast!), 'for by a single offering he has perfected for all time those who are sanctified' (Hebrews 10.14).

I have always found the doctrine of 'total depravity' (correctly understood) strangely comforting in this respect. Sin has affected every part of human nature and we cannot please God in our own strength. As this relates to counting and measuring, we remember that 'our work is affected by sin, our knowledge is incomplete, our capabilities are limited and our motives are mixed.'[45] Nothing we do will ever be effective in the sense that Jesus' death on the cross was effective – 'by his one oblation of himself once offered, a full, perfect and sufficient sacrifice, oblation and satisfaction for the sins of the whole world', as the Book of Common Prayer puts it. And yet there is much stress in business, education, even the arts, on whether return for resource or effort constitutes a good investment.

I know that resources are scarce and we need to be good stewards of them, so assessing the effectiveness of something or other is often necessary. But the trouble is that not everything in the kingdom can be measured in this way and 'creating and maintaining a culture of grace instead of a culture of fear is vital.'[46]

The Resourcing Ministerial Education Task Group was formed in 2015 to enable to Church of England to develop a strategy to 'develop proposals for the most *effective* use of resources for ministerial education' (emphasis mine).[47] There was much talk of what constitutes 'value for money' in preparing ministers for ordination and other ministries.[48] There is, of course, some need for this. I needed to know as a college principal that I had successfully trained ministers who would do the task the Church needed them to do. There are learning outcomes and criteria, and students must show evidence of having met them. But the trouble is that the kingdom of God is not often like that. Is forgiveness 'effective'? Is grace good 'value for money'?

The creep of economic criteria for the evaluation of educational institutions is pervasive. In an interview with the *Church Times*, Ian McFarland, Regius Professor of Divinity at Cambridge, laments the burden placed on higher education institutions by the requirements of the Higher Education Funding Council (now the Office for Students):

The emphasis in Britain on "value for money" – which really means about economic return on a degree – seems absolutely poisonous for meaningful education, especially in divinity . . . Universities at their best train people to be curious about what they don't know and self-confident about engaging with new ideas.[49]

Most higher education colleges now have to submit returns related to the future salaries of their graduates in order to enable students to choose where to study, based on how a certain qualification will maximize their earnings potential. What is true of education more widely is also creeping in to the education institutions of the Church, with possibly a little less emphasis on earnings.

The trouble with using words such as 'effectiveness' in relation to ministry, still less 'value for money', is that we might begin to see the work of God as a business proposition, where little trainee ministers are moved along an assembly line of lectures and learning outcomes until they become 'effective' units of Church growth and hence, more importantly, of income generation to bolster the flagging economy of the Church. The report by the Faith and Order Commission into senior leadership, asks the pertinent question:

> Do the expectations currently surrounding leaders focus on effectiveness and 'success' in ways that undermine a distinctive Christian understanding of action, in which one's action is a gift that one receives more than it is something that one achieves; in which there can be no effectiveness without grace; and in which failure is one source of God's blessing?[50]

I am always heartened by Jesus' own telling of the Parable of the Sower (Matthew 13.1–23; Mark 4.1–20; Luke 8.4–15). Not only does it point up the apparent 'ineffectiveness' of even Jesus' own teaching ministry (an encouragement to anyone who, albeit human and not divine, has ever felt the same frustrations), but it also highlights the fact that, in the kingdom of God, the fragile work of ministry will often move slowly, unpredictably, unevenly and in unquantifiable ways. We are simply to be obedient in broadcasting the good news widely, and to leave the hidden, unseen work of germinating the seeds to God. Any 'success' in the parable is the success of the word of God in the reign of heaven.[51]

Let anyone who has ears, listen!

4

Comparing

We do not dare to classify or compare ourselves with some of those who commend themselves. But when they measure themselves by one another, and compare themselves with one another, they do not show good sense. (2 Corinthians 10.12)

Tell me, what is it you plan to do with your one wild and precious life?
(Mary Oliver, 'The summer day')[1]

What is it to you?

In preparation for writing this book, I did some research into how churches describe themselves on their websites. It was quite revealing. All of them speak of themselves in glowing terms: 'large and vibrant', 'active and vibrant', 'lively, growing', 'large and diverse', 'passionate'. Now, I do love a good mission statement, but I do wonder if what is going on here is less about description and more about standing out, being distinguishable from all the other churches? Is it about branding, image, and, dare I say it, competition?

One of the tasks of leadership is to speak well of the institution, organization, church, that you lead, to show it in its best light, to speak positive possibilities into being. What is true of churches is no less true of commercial enterprises, cafés, schools and colleges. Such self-defining statements can either be inspiring and attractive or unrealistic, untrue and simply designed to show the church in the best light in comparison with the church down the road. There is a great pressure for leaders to 'show and tell' in winsome ways that not only let people know what their thing is all about, but also help them to think that they might want to be part of it.

Secretly I long to see a set of church vision statements that describe the churches more honestly and realistically: 'St Botolph's: We're getting there slowly'; St Mungo's: A bit c**p, but never mind'; 'St Dionysus: We're not dead yet!' (preferably said in a Monty Python voice). A blog post encouraging a refocus on good governance as opposed to whizzy leadership asks:

> Developing a 'compelling vision' supported by a vision, mission statement and strap-line is exciting, perhaps even intoxicating, but are such activities in and of themselves a little bit hollow and, maybe even vacuous? Can corporate visions, mission statements and strap-lines become the very things capable of hoisting 'leaders' on their own petard?[2]

As with 'ambition', so also with 'leadership', my belief is that it need not be a dirty word for Christians, and we can reclaim and reinhabit both concepts for appropriate Christ-focused use for the glory of God. However, the word 'leadership' is by its very nature a comparative word. If someone is going to be the leader, others will have to be 'followers', or at least 'not leaders', or 'not so much leaders', or 'not the same kind of leaders'. And comparison is tricky for Christians. When the Bible tells us to compare ourselves with others, it does so in supposedly inverse ways: 'Whoever wants to be first must be last of all and servant of all' (Mark 9.35); '[do not] think of yourself more highly than you ought to think' (Romans 12.3); 'in humility regard others as better than yourselves' (Philippians 2.3).

When it comes to ambition and success, we do not exist in a vacuum. Many leaders struggle with notions of self-worth *in relation to others*. It is so easy to compare oneself with the church down the road, the vicar down the road, the leader down the road. It's not limited to the Church either. I spoke to a young teacher who was concerned that she wasn't good enough in comparison with her other colleagues in the science department, that she was somehow letting the team down.

The tendency to compare ourselves with others is a natural human instinct. It starts when we're about three years old and I notice that that kid's shoes have flashing lights on, and mine don't, and it doesn't stop. And it's found no less in Christian leaders than it is in anyone else.

We live in a culture that encourages us to do this. Social media gives us instant access to the lives of others, which leads us, consciously or otherwise, to compare what we are doing, what our homes look like, what our kids are up to, what holidays we go on, what our churches are doing, with everyone else (but without the realistic, perspective-giving, sobering lens of the things we would never post on Facebook, that is the reality of most of the rest of life). I know I do it. I host an event that gets a good turnout and I post it online, usually with pictures (taken at the most 'effective' angle to show larger numbers of people – yes, numeritis), plus captions that show feigned humble surprise at how well things have gone – 'Great to see soooo many people at [*insert name of event*] this evening'. Much as I love to look at what friends have been up to and keep in touch with my nearest and dearest, and those I consider acquaintances (all 1,042 of them), I am also tempted to compare my life with theirs in ways whereby my life invariably comes off worse. On Twitter we document our lives and thoughts in moment-by-moment chunks of 280 characters or fewer. ('Fewer'. It's 'fewer'. Not 'less'.) As we read and see what others are doing and hear the exciting places they are going, the spectre that our meagre lot may be less significant or less fun than theirs is ever present.

Learning to live well with comparison is a key skill of leadership. The problem is that we don't always get it modelled very well for us by those we see in positions of power. It's fascinating, if somewhat sobering, to take a look through Donald Trump's Tweets and see how many of them are about how good he is in comparison to anyone else, his status, his policies, his position, his achievements. What Donald Trump cares about most is not that he is a successful American president, but that he is *the most* successful American president. Ever. He doesn't just want to win. He wants to win big. He doesn't just want his ratings to be good. He wants them to be the best. When White House strategist Steve Bannon featured on the cover of *Time Magazine*, Trump was purportedly annoyed because that was one more edition where he was not. For him, success is a zero-sum game. Like many celebrities, what Trump fears most is being ignored, insignificant, nobody. Consider this from Madonna (the singer, not the mother of Jesus) in an interview with *Vanity Fair* magazine:

> My drive in life comes from a fear of being mediocre. That is always pushing me. I push past one spell of it and discover myself as a special human being but then I feel I am still mediocre and uninteresting unless I do something else. Because even though I have become Somebody, I still have to prove that I am Somebody. My struggle has never ended and I guess it never will.[3]

Madonna's biggest fear is mediocrity. The thing she seeks to avoid is being exactly the same as everyone else. It is so easy to become obsessed with oneself, not only with oneself per se, but also with oneself *in relation to others*. Perhaps this is what lay behind the disciples' question to Jesus in Matthew 18, 'Who is the greatest in the kingdom of heaven?' (Matthew 18.1). Not simply, 'Who is great?', but 'Who is the greatest?' We can scoff at their naivety, but there is real temptation in Christian ministry to constantly wonder how you are doing in relation to someone else – your training incumbent or your colleague or your friends or the other people in your peer group. Whose church is the biggest? Who has the most people on their Alpha course? Who is the most effective leader? Who is the greatest?

One of my very favourite scenes in the whole Bible is that wonderful moment in John 21 when Jesus is sitting with Peter on the beach after the resurrection. They eat breakfast, and then Jesus asks Peter, 'Do you love me?' Peter answers, 'Yes, Lord, you know that I love you' (three times). Jesus commissions him to feed his sheep and there is a beautiful moment, between them, eye to eye, man to man, friend to friend, Saviour to saved. Then, Peter looks out the corner of his eye and notices John loitering nearby and asks, 'Lord, what about him?' (John 21.21). 'Can I feed your sheep more than he feeds them?' (I paraphrase). Jesus replies, 'If it is my will that he remain until I come, what is that to you? Follow me!' (John 21.22).

Don't look at what the person over there is doing . . .

You follow me.

A culture of comparison

Comparing ourselves with others can provide either inspiration or inferiority. It is a natural human tendency to want to compare ourselves with others so we need to be cautious about where we focus our attention, who we aim to emulate and with what end. There is power in comparing ourselves with the right people, for the right reasons. One writer on happiness suggests that rather than publishing a Rich List every year, we should publish a Top Taxpayers' list, in order to inspire greater altruism in our society: 'If we know that we are hardwired to compete and to compare, then let's use this to write social narratives that we can all benefit from.'[4]

So let's name some of the pitfalls for comparison that might become points of temptation for Christian leaders to compare themselves negatively with others. These factors are most linked to Church ministry, but will have points of comparability with other vocations and work contexts too.

I have noticed among Church leaders (including myself, I'm ashamed to admit) a tendency to exaggerate when speaking about the numbers involved in their college/ministry/

Alpha course, rounding everything up by just a few in order to make things look and sound just a little bit better, a little bit more fruitful, a tad more successful. It is a particular form of 'numeritis'. Hence eight people attending a course becomes 'nearly 10', 51 people at church becomes 'over 50'. I have known some serial offenders so bad that that when they left a parish to moved on to pastures new, the numbers belonging to their church appeared to drop considerably almost overnight, not because anyone actually left, but simply because the next incumbent was more honest and accurate with the counting. In a talk I heard from one especially bad offender the number of people at a speaking engagement he was recounting practically doubled during the telling of the story. 'Evangelasticity' is a phrase coined by Martin Saunders to describe the tendency for church ministers to exaggerate for effect, especially when describing numbers: 'Tens become hundreds; hundreds become thousands.'[5]

Yet Jesus told a tale of rejoicing over *just one* sheep that was lost and then found. He didn't even try to make it sound like it was two.

'Church porn'

It is normal to show off the organization or group we are associated with. Most of my social media feed is taken up with pictures of excellent things my college, my church, my networks, have been up to that I am proud of and think worth sharing with others. I want to show these things in their best light. When I took up my post as principal of Trinity College one of the first things I did was to oversee a rebranding exercise, to help the college to refresh its image and the way it was perceived, resulting in a new website, new publicity materials, a new logo and strapline. I love all that stuff. I enjoy looking at the websites and 'shop fronts' of different colleges, churches, dioceses and organizations. When I come across a good one I think, 'Oh, now, that's nice. That's different. That's appealing.' There is nothing wrong with this, unless it begins to cause in me uncontrollable bouts of envy – 'I wish my website was that good. I wish I'd thought of that publicity tactic. I wish my Instagram pictures looked like that.' Someone once referred to surfing other churches' publicity materials as looking at 'church porn'. You know you shouldn't look because afterwards it doesn't make you feel good about yourself. But you can't help it. You sneak a look at the website of others churches or organizations, and you wish it was yours. You admire it. You think about it. You dwell on it.

There has recently been, across the Church of England, a spate of church plants, using models developed by (and often with ministry staff from) Holy Trinity Brompton. These plants have been set up and funded by the aforementioned Strategic Development Funding and other sources of income. They have largely been very 'successful' and have very quickly grown in numbers and influence in their local communities. Where these have been introduced and set up well, with effective local communication, this has been received as a good development. In a few places, however, a certain amount of resentment from existing churches and church leaders has resulted. Nobody disputes the need for new initiatives to bring new people into the kingdom of God, but the relationships around the starting up of these plants are not always straightforward. The church-planters believe they are simply being ambitious for God, succeeding in the work of mission in that area, especially focusing on young adults and students. But other churches in the area may experience it as competition, 'moving into my patch', market forces, church-hopping, one church winning over another. Although there are more than enough people who are not yet Christians to go round many, many churches, the presence of a highly attractive new Holy-Trinity-Brompton-branded church moving into your area can feel very much like a takeover bid. I was speaking to a church leader who very candidly admitted that sometimes he worries that if he sees someone down the road having success in one form or another, he struggles to rejoice, because there might be only so much success to go round, and he might be the one to miss out. It does not help when, as a Church, we inadvertently encourage this view that there is a certain class of super-clergy, more likely to be successful than others.

The 'talent pool'

Henri Nouwen paints a poignant picture of the constant feeling experienced by many Church leaders of needing to prove their worth in the light of others', and their own, expectations – to be ministerial superstars:

> Many of us feel like failed tightrope walkers who discovered that we did not have the power to draw thousands of people, that we could not make many conversions, that we did not have the talents to create beautiful liturgies,

that we were not as popular with the youth, the young adults, or the elderly as we had hoped, that we were not as able to respond to the needs of our people as we had expected. But most of us still feel that, ideally, we should have been able to do it all and do it successfully. Stardom and individual heroism, which are such obvious aspects of our competitive society, are not at all alien to the church.[6]

An early element of the Renewal and Reform programme was a realization that Something Needed to be Done about the calibre of ministers presenting themselves for 'wider' Church leadership, and those being prepared to take up 'senior' leadership roles. The basic premise is that those who are considered to have potential for senior leadership in the Church (not just bishops, but archdeacons, deans and theological institution principals) are spotted and given extra support and training on the Strategic Leadership Development Programme (SLDP). The language of the original report in which this idea was put forward used the terms 'talent pool' and 'talent management' and is packed full of comparatives and superlatives.[7] The word 'exceptional' occurs 16 times in a 30-page report. Those chosen for this programme should be 'clergy of exceptional leadership potential' and 'the strongest performer in their peer group'. The cohort should be made up of 'a small number of outstanding individuals, who demonstrate exceptional performance and potential over a sustained period of time', who 'consistently demonstrate exceptional potential against all agreed criteria'. The word 'performance' occurs 20 times, collocated with 'high-', 'strong-', 'exceptional-' and 'outstanding-'.

It is all about those who stand out from the crowd. I know many exceptional, outstanding leaders, but I don't know many who would be keen to describe themselves using this kind of language.

Jennifer and Gianpiero Petriglieri, who study and work with 'future leaders', have identified a phenomenon they have termed 'the talent curse'.[8] They show how identifying and lauding young leaders as 'star performers' can actually be detrimental to their future development, causing them to burn out trying to live up to the expectations placed on them:

> In most cases, these managers and professionals have been accurately identified as star performers and fast learners. But often, placement on a fast track doesn't speed up their growth as leaders in the organization, as it's meant to do. Instead, it either pushes them out the door or slows them down—thwarting their development, decreasing their engagement, and hurting their performance.

Far from being an incentive, being identified as foremost among their peers can actually be a curse, as 'the qualities that made them special to begin with – those that helped them excel and feel engaged – tend to get buried'. There can exist a lethal combination of idealization and identification as 'others idealise their talent as a defence against the company's uncertain future, and then the high potentials identify with that image, shouldering the uncertainty themselves'. The levels of burnout and dropout among such leaders are high. The Petriglieris land some of the blame at the feet of their managers for not supporting the young leaders in their new task. They cite a leader named Laura who burns out after taking on greater responsibility:

> They did not maliciously withdraw support, but they didn't encourage her to seek it, either. They never invited her to take it a little easier or told her that she shouldn't expect to get everything right. And so they reinforced her modus operandi.

Although the Church is not a primarily business organization, it is easy to recognize some parallels. The young leader who has shown potential in mission and church leadership gets invited to be on various groups and committees, becomes central to the strategy of the diocese, is asked to plant another church, and the levels of expectation rise. One such young leader in exactly this position confessed to me to feeling bowed down by the weight of expectation placed upon him that he, and he alone, would be the one to reverse the trend of the diocese's declining church attendance figures.

The language of the 'talent pool' with its 'outstanding individuals' could be particularly problematic for female leaders. It is well documented that men will apply for jobs if they fulfil most of the criteria on the job description, whereas many women will not apply unless they think they can prove competence in *all* the criteria. Kate Coleman refers to a particularly female trait which she calls 'the sin of hiding', or 'shrinking to fit', by which women tend to downplay their gifts and abilities in order to be accepted by the wider group. The narrative that a woman should not assert herself above others ('because they're good at collaborative leadership, aren't they?') leads some women to shy away from taking up rightful authority, based entirely on an accurate assessment of their skills, abilities and vocation. During question times after lectures or at conferences, I have observed time after time women prefacing their questions with an apologies – 'I hesitate to ask this question for fear of revealing my ignorance but . . .' – and then proceeding to ask perfectly intelligent questions. Shrinking to fit might also involve not taking a lead where it is right to do so, not taking initiatives for fear of failure and in case others might not like us, underplaying or downplaying one's own contribution or significance, and putting any successes down to other factors, rather than taking rightful credit for them.

There may also be an added burden for women who choose to put their heads above the parapets and pursue their (godly) ambitions to leadership. Nancy Beach calls it 'the freight of being iconic.'[9] This is the burden women can often feel to excel and be exceptional in their chosen field, not only because they want to represent themselves well but because they are aware of somehow representing the whole of womankind. This is particularly true when women are still the minority in a particular role. So when I became bishop of Penrith, I was aware of wanting to do the job well (for all sorts of very good reasons) but also because I knew that the headlines on the day of my announcement all alluded to 'Cumbria's first woman bishop' and I wanted to show that a woman can do as good a job as a man. Several recent studies into gender difference in leadership find that women are better at achieving results and are, in many respects, more 'effective' in their leadership than men.[10] This could be, however, because they work their socks off to counter negative perceptions of themselves and by others. When women were presented with the results of one such study[11] and asked to suggest reasons why women had been rated so highly as leaders, they said: 'We need to work harder then men to prove ourselves'; 'We feel the constant pressure to never make a mistake and to continually prove our value to the organisation.' There is a perception among women leaders that we have to do well not just because we want to do well, but because we want to do well *as women*.

The Church of England senior leadership report I mentioned earlier (the Green Report) identifies a series of 'contraindications' to a person being identified as ready to dive into the talent pool: 'aspects of the individual that interfere with growth thus detracting from potential'. These include a 'lack of time commitment' and 'family issues', which could give the impression that one can only be in the talent pool if one is free of such burdensome things. That is likely to affect women who are often working hard in parishes with little extra support so have limited spare capacity to engage in such a programme, and women who are likely to have family responsibilities over and above their ministry commitments. Kate Coleman identifies 'the disease to please'[12] that can lead to difficulty in women knowing, and letting others know, where boundaries begin and end and recognizing how and when to say 'yes' and 'no'. Women may be more ambivalent about setting limits, due to social pressure and a desire to gain the approval of others. This may not bode well for women church leaders and their emotional health, playing into a tendency in some women to overwork and to neglect appropriate time and self-care boundaries.

There is also a sense in which all this talk of the 'brightest and best' should grate against all of us, not only women, because it is in tension with the kind of Christ-like leadership we are all called to, following a Saviour who 'though he was in the form of God, did not regard equality with God as something to be exploited, but emptied himself' (Philippians 2.6–7). When comparing ourselves with others, as we inevitably do, perhaps we need to stop and think with whom we would like to be compared. Who do we look up to? Who do we have as role models? Possibly we should not include among that number those who work themselves into the ground in order to 'consistently and intensively sustain success.'[13]

Feeding the approval monster

So it seems that the key is once again to assess motivation, and to ask the question, why do I compare myself with others? Is it because I want to learn something from someone I respect and wish to emulate? Or is it because I am not sure of my own self-worth and need to 'benchmark' myself against another person? Why do I care so much what others think of me? Is that where I go to gain my sense of approval? Am I constantly comparing myself with others needing affirmation to bolster my own sense of self-worth?

Am I an approval junkie?

Paul asks similar questions in Galatians 1.10: 'Am I now seeking human approval, or God's approval? Or am I trying to please people? If I were still pleasing people, I would not be a servant of Christ.' This is a good quotation for ambitious leaders to have ever before them. I have begun to think of the need for approval from others as having a kind of interior monster who thrives on words of approval, gets very hungry and demands to be fed. Because, much as we don't like to admit it, those with a high aptitude for performance have an interior approval monster who is very, very greedy. The best description of this tendency comes in *Lake Woebegone Days* by Garrison Keillor, who paints the picture of a character who is obsessed with approval:

> Under this thin veneer of modesty lies a monster of greed. I drive away from faint praise, beating my little chest, waiting to be named Sun-God, King of America, Idol of Millions, Bringer of Fire, The Great Haji, Thun-Dar the Boy Giant. As pathetic as it sounds, sometimes when I'm offered sincere affirmation, I don't want to say, 'Thanks, glad you liked it.' I want to say, 'Rise, my people. Remove your faces from the carpet, stand, look me in the face.'[14]

John Ortberg writes about how when he stands up to speak on Sunday morning, there are two voices in his head:

> the congregation hears my voice, but I hear another, more confusing voice in my head. It's also my voice. Sometimes it shouts, Thus saith the Lord. But at other times, more often than I care to admit, the voice is less prophetic. What will they think of me? the voice wonders.[15]

So perhaps when we feel the approval monster calling to be fed, we need to remind ourselves again that we are 'living for an audience of one'[16]; the only person whose opinion really matters – Jesus. It is his will I am doing, and his approval I seek. As Paul says:

> Let no one boast about human leaders. For all things are yours, whether Paul or Apollos or Cephas or the world or life or death or the present or the future – all belong to you, and you belong to Christ, and Christ belongs to God.
> (1 Corinthians 3.21)

We can have confidence, but a confidence that is based not on our own performance, but on who we are in Christ. We don't have to prove ourselves because Jesus has done all the proving that was ever needed. We are accepted, validated, recommended, meet the standard, fulfil the requirements, only because of what Jesus has done for us on the cross. All God's final judgement rested upon him on our behalf and he was not found wanting. So Paul is able to say:

> with me it is a very small thing that I should be judged by you or by any human court. *I do not even judge myself.* I am not aware of anything against myself, but I am not thereby acquitted. It is the Lord who judges me.
> (1 Corinthians 4.3–7; emphasis mine)

We don't pass or fail by human judgement, even our own judgement of ourselves. Imagine being released from always having to wonder what people are thinking of you or how you're doing, from having to connect every conversation, event, meeting, encounter, to yourself and your own feelings. Thomas Merton said, 'A humble man can do great things with an uncommon perfection because he is no longer concerned about accidentals, like his own interests and his own reputation, and therefore he no longer needs to waste his efforts in defending them.'[17]

How to subdue the approval monster

1 Don't be like Diotrephes

Beware of anything that rates the followers of Christ in relation to one another. John's third letter (3 John) is the shortest book in the New Testament, coming in at around 219 words. It is written to someone called Gaius, who is commended for providing hospitality to travelling missionaries, apparently against the advice of a character in the church named Diotrephes, who is described thus: 'I have written something to the church; but Diotrephes, *who likes to put himself first*, does not acknowledge our authority' (3 John 1.9; emphasis mine). No one knows much about Diotrephes except his desire for superiority. It could be that he was one of the first monarchical bishops or he was in conflict with John over who was in charge of the church. What is clear is that Diotrephes wanted to be top-dog. The word used for him is *philoproteuo* (proto – first, leader, philo – love) and describes a kind of hankering after pre-eminence. One translation could be 'ambitious for distinction'. Diotrephes seems to resent John's oversight or influence in the church. He wants to be the only one to call the shots, and does what he can to remain in charge; 'Diotrephes is a standing warning against the danger of *confusing personal ambition with zeal for the cause of the gospel*' (emphasis mine).[18]

Whenever I experience success of any kind, particularly when on my watch the graphs do appear to be going in the right direction, whenever I position myself strategically or find myself ambitious to achieve – whatever that might look like – I need to ask myself, 'Am I infected with the spirit of Diotrephes?' Is this because I'm doing well at what God has called me to do or do I love to be first? Am I confusing personal ambition with zeal for the cause of the gospel?

2 Be self-aware, but not self-obsessed

Leaders need to be aware of themselves, and their own strengths and weaknesses, and sometimes to communicate these appropriately to others.

In all areas of life and work we're required to take time to reflect on who we are, what our skills and aptitudes are, what we're good at, what we're less good at, how we perceive various aspects of the demands and requirements of our current role. This is certainly true in theological education. At Trinity, students have to fill in a twice-a-term self-reflection form to help them to take stock of developing knowledge, gifts, skills and spiritual growth and to identify areas for particular further development. Ordained ministers likewise undergo regular Ministerial Development Reviews, to enable them to 'reflect on and grow in their role . . . to encourage and develop them in ministry', using development tools 'designed to provide ordained ministers with a broad view of how their ministry is experienced and to clarify what they should be concentrating on'.[19]

Self-awareness is the order of the day. All that stuff is necessary and good. Paul's instruction to his young protégé

Timothy was to 'Pay close attention to yourself and to your teaching; continue in these things, for in doing this you will save both yourself and your hearers' (1 Timothy 4.16).

We need to know our strengths and we need to be aware of our weaknesses.[20] Being aware of our limitations as well as our strengths makes us more likely to attribute any successes to the help and guidance of God. In a sermon, Augustine exhorts, 'Let us administer reproof, certainly – but first of all to ourselves. You wish to reprove your neighbour, and nothing is a nearer neighbour to you than yourself. Why go far away? You have yourself right there in front of you.'[21] It is certainly true that some leaders need to pay far more attention to their own sense of self, inner well-being and spiritual health than they often allow time for in a life of busy demands.

However, there also comes a point at which you need to forget yourself. Jones and Armstrong identify the issue of leaders who have been so encouraged into self reflection, via 'therapeutic' approaches, that they become overly obsessed with themselves:

Self-absorbed ministry issues from a pastor's lack of Christian character. Whether a matter of excessive estimation of one's own importance or a sense of weakness and insecurity, everything resolves around the pastor's need to be the focus of attention and affirmation.[22]

Perhaps the key to this lies in the other half of the encounter between Jesus and Peter on the beach in John 21. Jesus not only asks Peter to take charge of the welfare of his flock but he also alludes to what will happen to him in later life:

Very truly, I tell you, when you were younger, you used to fasten your own belt and to go wherever you wished. But when you grow old, you will stretch out your hands, and someone else will fasten a belt around you and take you where you do not wish to go.
(John 21.18)

In other words, whether he likes it or not, Peter will go from leader to the one being led. Nouwen says:

The way of the Christian leader is not the way of upward mobility in which our world has invested so much, but the way of downward mobility ending on the cross . . . Here we touch the most important quality of Christian leadership in the future. It is not a leadership of power and control, but a leadership of powerlessness in which the suffering servant of God, Jesus Christ is made manifest.[23]

Of course, we must be somewhat wary of always associating ministry with suffering. Particularly those who have been disempowered and oppressed do not need to be told that they just have to learn to suffer quietly. But for any leader who is a Christian seeking to follow the way of Christ, there comes a point where self must become secondary to the One who suffered and enters into the experience of all suffering.

3 Beware the lure of 'celebrity'

When I was exploring whether I had a call to ordained ministry, I took several personality tests to help understand myself better. One of the things they showed me is that I quite like performing. I get energy from it. I enjoy it. I'm OK at it. All right, I'm relatively good at it. I come from a family of amateur dramatists and I have always had a love of theatre, enjoy speaking and acting, and have grown in confidence in public 'performance'. For a while I thought this precluded me from being a vicar, and that perhaps I should pursue a life on the stage instead. That was until a wise friend pointed out to me how much of 'professional' ministry was, in fact, performance. Standing in a pulpit to preach, standing at the front of a church to lead a service, welcoming a group of visitors, hosting a pub discussion on the relative merits of religion, even standing up to take a funeral with confidence and calmness when everything inside you wants to curl up on the front pew with the bereaved relatives and cry and wail. There is a lot of acting in ministry. I suspect the same is true of leaders in many other professions too. The good teachers I can remember at school were those who held the attention of the class and had a certain 'something' that made learning captivating and enjoyable. I would go so far as to say that all good leadership involves some degree of performance. By this I don't mean being something other than genuinely oneself and simply acting a part but, rather, using all the gifts of character and skills of presentation and engagement to make the most of any leadership situation in which one finds oneself. Along with this aptitude for performance that many Christian leaders exhibit comes the associated praise and criticism that all actors enjoy (or not).

The other day my son went to a party where one of the people there asked him that fateful question about whether he was related to me. We don't have a common surname and it happens quite often. My son came home and said, in that slightly amused and mocking way that only teenagers can manage, 'Mum, did you know you're some kind of minor Christian celebrity?' I am ashamed to admit to you how much I enjoyed that comment. I am known? People have heard of me? I must have significance! (Albeit in some incredibly insignificant, minor, B-list, infinitesimally small Evangelical, churchy-focused kind of a way.) But those people don't really *know* me. I need to heed the warning that:

> The people who are exposed only to your public ministry persona, your books or Internet blogs, and your voice when it is in a conference or on a dvd are functionally incapable of giving you an accurate view of yourself. You must take their congratulatory words as well meant but lacking accuracy and therefore spiritual helpfulness.[24]

Or as Jesus said, 'Woe to you when all speak well of you' (Luke 6.26).

It is right to focus on being the best we can be, using our God-given gifts and wholeheartedly pursuing his calling on our lives. But the trouble is that this can all too easily collapse into a search for recognition quite unworthy of Christian discipleship. For good reason, Gregory the Great reminds his clergy not to be 'diverted by the commendations of others.'[25]

Over this past few years, the Church and society as a whole has been shaken by some very high-profile 'falls from grace'. Household names and childhood entertainers have been found to be covert abusers. Formerly respected and influential Church leaders have been uncovered as, at best, unwise in monitoring their personal boundaries and, at worst, as manipulative and devious sexual harassers. Under the #MeToo campaign, the world is finally waking up to the need for more rigorous systems of preventing, detecting and responding to abuse and harassment and, consequently, several people previously thought untouchable have been rightly knocked off their celebrity pedestals. The lure is no less for Christian leaders. Andy Crouch addresses the phenomenon of Christian celebrity, which carries added dangers, warning that 'celebrity combines the old distance of power with what seems like its exact opposite extraordinary intimacy, or at least a bewitching simulation of intimacy.'[26] Crouch, who because of his writing and speaking is fairly well known, outlines the steps he takes to limit his own sense of celebrity. He has a close support network of friends who are able to speak accountably into his life (amusingly called The Eulogisers, as these are the ones who will offer the eulogy at his funeral). He also says, 'At events that use name tags, I wear one.'

I love the story told at the end of Henri Nouwen's book *In the Name of Jesus* in which he recounts being asked to speak at a high-profile event, at which he was already well known, and taking with him one of his fellow members of the L'Arche community, Bill, who has learning disabilities. Bill refused to take a back seat and insisted on sharing the podium with Nouwen. Nouwen tells movingly how Bill won the hearts of everyone there and helped Nouwen himself to see the real truth that 'most likely much of what I said would not be long remembered, but that Bill and I doing it together would not be easily forgotten.'[27]

We need other people to stop us abusing our power and to see our real worth. We need accountability, good governance and friends, not just followers. If someone said to me, 'I'd follow you anywhere', I'd worry.

A lot.

4 Understand humility correctly

Humility is undoubtedly one of the most important dispositions for Christ-like leadership. However, humility must be understood correctly. C. S. Lewis said:

> If anyone would like to acquire humility, I can, I think, tell him the first step. The first step is to realise that one is proud. And a biggish step, too. At least, nothing whatever can be done before it. If you think you are not conceited, it means you are very conceited indeed.[28]

In other words, we need to develop less self-absorption. The trouble is that some leaders have mistaken true humility for fear and self-loathing. For some leaders, what might be spoken of ostensibly as self-sacrifice and humility might actually be thinly disguised anxiety and fear. Much has been written recently about the need for leaders to show vulnerability. That may be so, and for some, perhaps of a certain generation or, dare I say, a certain gender, there is a need to be given permission to speak of struggles and weaknesses. However, many leaders I know, particularly female leaders, are quite good at speaking the language of humility and vulnerability.

After I took up my post as principal of Trinity College, we developed a set of community promises, based on the Beatitudes. Each promise is condensed to a single word – courage, diversity, hospitality, service and so on. And the first is humility. I had preached my very first sermon as principal on humility and it had been posted up on the college website afterwards, upon which I received a fairly angry response from a female past student who had struggled with self-esteem issues. Didn't I realize that talking about humility was dangerous for women? Too many women do not have a well-developed sense of their own self-worth, and talking too much about humility leads them to fail to see themselves as worthy of anything. This is not what is meant by real humility. Only those with a firmly understood and developed sense of their own identity in Christ have the strength and purpose to 'humble *themselves*' (Matthew 23.12; Luke 14.11; emphasis mine) (the word in Greek is reflexive – no one can do the humbling for you).

There are some leaders who have been afraid to step out into those places God is calling them or to greater level of responsibility or to a role of greater prominence, because they are afraid to be seen as pushy or proud or arrogant. They may be tempted to hide behind the language of humility and vulnerability because they are actually rather scared, but saying we're being humble sounds better. One blog from a female leader says, 'Many of us internalize false messages about the nature of meekness, humility, and femininity that cause us to self-sabotage and devalue our own callings.'[29]

To confuse reticence to fully own our authority with true humility is a dangerous path to take. In his book tracing the surprising factors that lead to success (or otherwise), Malcolm Gladwell points to the fact that, in the case of several air crashes, there had been an unwillingness on the part of junior pilots to speak up in dangerous situations, even when they had the superior knowledge to do so, for fear of usurping the status of their more senior colleagues, with disastrous results.[30] Similarly, some mistakes made during surgery might have been avoided by the presence of systems (such as checklists) designed to enable junior staff to have the courage to challenge senior colleagues at an earlier stage, where they saw impending mistakes happening. Such checks 'helped flatten hierarchies and identify dangerous omissions that might otherwise have been missed.'[31] Now, not many of us will find ourselves piloting aircraft or removing organs, but a fear of directly owning and inhabiting our own authority, and claiming 'humility' as a way of covering for our inhibition, may lead to crashes, or tragic mistakes, of another sort.

Fear is not the same as humility. Don't cloak fear in the acceptable Christian jargon of humility and self-sacrifice. Before the face of God, learn what for you, is fear, and what is appropriate vulnerability – and know the difference.

Because you're worth it.

As the Collect for the Fifth Sunday before Lent says:

> Almighty God,
> by whose grace alone we are accepted and
> called to your service;
> Strengthen us by your spirit
> and make us worthy of our calling;
> Through Jesus Christ our Lord, Amen.

5

Leadership in the image of the Trinity

WANTED: For small country heading in unknown direction at dangerous time LEADERSHIP. Applicants need to be available to start immediately.
(Nick Robinson's Tweet)[1]

A study in power and authority

Never before have we heard the word 'leadership' in the media quite as much as in the past few years. These have been tumultuous days in politics and the cry everywhere has been, 'We need [insert additional word here. Options: strong, decisive, clear] leadership!' But while people cry out for 'leadership', do they really know what they are asking for? What seems to be most at stake are questions about the nature of authority. Who has the authority to decide what happens? How do decisions get made, and by whom?

The 2015 Labour leadership contest highlighted the fact that even determining who chooses leaders is no simple matter. Jeremy Corbyn was elected by 'grass roots' party members, even as his own parliamentary colleagues expressed doubts. The election of Donald Trump to the Presidency of the USA, and his support, especially among white working-class voters, was largely portrayed as a reaction against the 'Washington elite' who had up until now called the shots. Michael Gove in his campaigning for the 2016 Brexit referendum questioned the wisdom of heeding the views of 'experts' in order to 'take back control' of the powers of decision-making. In a BBC documentary following the Brexit referendum, MP Ken Clarke offered his analysis of the outcome: 'The result was about . . . people who had been left behind and a ferocious dislike of the establishment and the political class in particular.'[2] More recently, as the Brexit negotiations rumble on, the back benches of Parliament have sought to exercise their authority over the government, while Theresa May spoke of a potential 'catastrophic and unforgivable breach of trust in our democracy'.[3]

What is happening to leadership?

My favourite Shakespeare play is *King Lear*, a fascinating study into what maintains civilization and order in society and in the human mind, and what keeps us from terrifying chaos. The play is all about the nature of authority – who has it, why and how it is lost. At the start of the play the banished Kent says to Lear (Act 1, Scene IV):

> Lear: Who wouldst thou serve?
> Kent: You.
> Lear: Dost thou know me, fellow?
> Kent: No, sir, but you have that in your countenance which I would fain call master.

Lear: What's that?
Kent: Authority.

Gradually through the play Lear gives away, mostly inadvertently and through his own weakness of character, all the power and authority he ever had, until he is left sitting mad and naked on the stage with his old friend blinded Gloucester.

It struck me how easy it would be for the Church of England to feel like that.

We made our entrance full of pomp and grandeur, all the trappings of power were ours, and over the years we find that we have given away our kingdom, our knights have been dismissed, we have lost our faculties (no pun intended), we've railed and ranted on the heathland of post-religious society shouting to anyone who will listen and now we sit weak and powerless lamenting that we are 'more sinned against than sinning'. And it's making us anxious. We need to rediscover what the true nature and source of our authority is, and how to use well any power we do have.

What goes for the Church as a whole also goes for its ministers/priests/leaders (I barely know which word to choose any more). By whose authority do we exist as a Church? Who gives us the right to speak about anything? Why should anyone listen? Where do we go for the answers? As we rediscover what it means to be 'King' in jail, lamenting the loss of our dearest treasures (OK, I'll stop the Lear imagery in a minute), we might be inclined to be content, with Lear (Act V, Scene III), to:

pray, and sing, and tell old tales, and laugh / At gilded butterflies, and hear poor rogues / Talk of court news;

and we'll talk with them too, / Who loses and who wins; who's in, who's out; / And take upon's the mystery of things, / As if we were God's spies.

What kind of authority?

In the early twentieth century, the sociologist Max Weber proposed a three-fold classification of legitimate authority – traditional, charismatic and 'rational-legal'.[4]

Traditional authority exists due to custom, because 'it has always been so'. It depends on established tradition or order. People with this kind of authority have often inherited it and can get things done because they have got an intrinsic mandate to do so. A good example would be the monarchy.

Rational-legal authority is the ability to get things done because you've been appointed or elected to do so. It's a bureaucratic legitimation, based on systems, selection procedures, expertise, ability to succeed in the job. Political elections and job interviews give this kind of authority.

Charismatic authority (not 'charismatic' in the sense of spiritual gifts, but of 'having charisma') influences by virtue of character, powers of persuasion, qualities, charm and rallying people to achieve things.

As leaders, even as leaders in the Church, there may be a sense in which we have all three of these kinds of authority. Certainly priests in the Church of England can still claim vestiges of a kind of traditional authority. We may not have been born into the role, but we certainly carry the trappings of establishment, for good or ill. There are lots of ways in which we can wear the '*it has always been so*' label. This may be a positive or a negative for the Church, depending on your view of establishment, but there is still very much a sense in many places of the Church of England being the 'traditional' Church.

Rational-legal authority underlies the authority given to anyone who has been interviewed, selected against criteria and chosen democratically to fulfil a role. Increasingly, this is the case for church leaders too. Gone are the days (largely) when the bishop simply tapped someone on the shoulder (usually someone sporting the same school/college tie) and shooed them into a vacant post. Patronage, while still holding meaning in the Church of England, is accompanied by legal and employment processes: advertising, job descriptions, appointment processes, common tenure, training, continual professional development, ministerial development reviews, appraisals, licenses. Some clergy and faith workers have even joined unions.

Many leaders will also have a certain sense of 'charismatic' authority. If you are in leadership, in any sphere it is likely that you will have certain qualities and personal characteristics that enable you to be the sort of person whom others listen and respond to. At least on a good day.

So what kind of authority can we expect to hold as Christian leaders, whether in the Church or in other fields such as business or education? What does leadership look like when we look at it theologically?

This is not an easy question to answer, because 'leadership' isn't really a very theological word. Of course, there are leaders and leadership in the Bible, but there is no nice stock of phrases or verses that we can lift out and say, 'There you are.

That's what the Bible says about leadership. Let's do that.' In fact, Jesus himself cautioned against using some of the common words around at the time to describe what he and his disciples were all about,

> You are not to be called 'rabbi', for you have one teacher, and you are all students. And call no one your 'father' on earth, for you have one Father – the one in heaven. Nor are you to be called 'instructors', for you have one instructor, the Messiah.
> (Matthew 23.8–12)

I wonder if today he might have added 'and be careful about being called "leaders", because there is only one Leader'.

The New Testament studiously avoids using the common words that were around at the time for leadership. The most common Greek word used for leader at the time was *archon* and yet this word is never used for leaders in the Church. Jesus himself is described in terms that many politicians would give their eye teeth for, 'as one who had authority' (Matthew 7.29), and yet when questioned about leadership, Jesus offers a very different way of thinking about it from the common currency of the time. The disciples, a bit like the Church today perhaps, were obsessed with notions of leadership and of who was going to be in charge, and they began to quarrel about it:

> A dispute also arose among them as to which one of them was to be regarded as the greatest. But he said to them, 'The kings of the Gentiles lord it over them;

and those in authority over them are called benefactors. But not so with you; rather the greatest among you must become like the youngest, and the leader like one who serves' (Luke 22.24–26).

But not so with you.

Notice that Jesus doesn't condemn human authority and leadership. He knows something like it is inevitable wherever there are people. Studies have consistently shown that wherever there are groups of people, power will eventually rest in the hands of one or a few. How, therefore, might we understand authority differently from the way in which others in the world – the equivalent of the 'kings of the Gentiles' – understand leadership?

Creator-shaped leadership: power and authority in the love of the Father

What does our authority as leaders and priests in God's Church look like when we view it from the perspective of the Father – God who created the heavens and the earth and holds all things in his hands?

One of the distinctive things about Christian leadership is that even though we might derive our earthly authority from all sorts of places, like being elected or authorized or certified or ordained, or having charisma, no human authority is ever absolute. Any authority we have as human leaders is derived from the ultimate authority of God. Even when Paul tells Christians to obey their earthly rulers – 'Let every person be subject to the governing authorities' – he also reminds them

that 'there is no authority except from God, and those authorities that exist have been instituted by God' (Romans 13.1).
Now, there are all sorts of questions we might want to ask
about whether one is supposed to obey authorities if they are
leading in ways opposed to God, but the point still stands: any
earthly leadership is always relative to that of God the Creator.
As Christians we always have another Head – Jesus Christ. As
the American Bishop Todd Hunter has said, that's the conundrum of Christian leadership – 'How do you lead people who
are supposed be following someone else?'

We need to remember this when much of the world around
us is frantic about leadership, and we might be tempted to join
in with the hype and allow others to try to make us into the
Messiah. That job is already taken.

However, human leadership is one of the ways God uses
to bless the world in his plan to reconcile the whole world to
himself.[5] God is the ultimate authority, the absolute leader, the
King, and Christians are his ambassadors sent by him to represent him in the world, and to bless the world in his name.
In 2 Corinthians 5 Paul writes that God has 'entrust[ed] the
message of reconciliation to us', before going on to say that 'we
are ambassadors for Christ, since God is making his appeal
through us; we entreat you on behalf of Christ, be reconciled
to God.' This could be a way of making sense of our 'traditional' authority in Weber's terms. We do inhabit an authority
born of right, but it is not worldly right and privilege. We have
inherited this authority, but it is not the divine right of kings,
but the mandate of the King of Kings who shares his authority
with his people – his ambassadors – for the purpose of blessing the world, in words and actions.[6]

It does not often feel in Christian ministry that we have much power or privilege, and although we're sent by the King of Kings, it often feels like jolly hard work. It most often feels like we need to earn the right to speak. Richard Neuhaus, in his book *Freedom for Ministry*, points out that being a Christian is a bit like having been appointed ambassador to a king whom other nations don't yet recognize: 'We are premature ambassadors, having arrived at court before the sovereignty of our king has been recognised. It is awkward, of course, and our authority is very much in question.'[7] One day, all the world will see and know our King but, until then, our authority as Christians will always be challenged. Perhaps this image helps to explain some of the tension and downright slog that being in Christian leadership brings sometimes, especially in tough contexts. Neuhaus goes on to say, 'We must resist the temptation to relieve the awkwardness by accepting a lesser authority from another kingdom.'[8] This calls for the ability to read the signs of the times and to recognize when we are being tempted to 'relieve the awkwardness', and who are the 'lesser kingdoms'. The values and tenets and characteristics of the kingdom of God are very different from those of the kingdoms of this world, and those who wish to mould their leadership in the shape of the upside-down kingdom of God will approach their task differently from those who seek the kind of leadership that the political and economic theories of our time and culture offers. When it comes to approaching theories of leadership, we must truly 'test everything; hold fast to what is good' (1 Thessalonians 5.21). We are premature ambassadors, confidently representing our King, resisting the temptation to accept the power of a lesser authority, despite the awkwardness.

As an example, Church of England clergy are not paid a salary. They receive a stipend, which is intended not as payment for work done, but expenses given to free a person from having to work for a salary in order to carry out ministry. Church of England clergy are not subject to the same employment laws as other professions (because they receive a stipend and not a salary, they are not employed) and so, in 2011, the Church of England introduced a terms of service framework that offers clergy some rights, while also placing them under certain obligations. Slowly, and possibly rightly in some respects, ordained ministry is coming to be seen as a professional job alongside other jobs. We are beginning to see more and more roles being offered to clergy as jobs, not offices, with salaries and other benefits, with set hours to be worked and with levels of responsibility 'benchmarked' against other jobs.

This may not be a bad thing in itself, but it serves as an example of the values and structures of 'another kingdom', the world of employment rights, rather than the world of ministry, working its way into the Church. How do you benchmark prayer or work out how many hours to spend with the dying or clock off after the Sunday service or evaluate the level of responsibility of a priest with 12 rural parishes no one has ever heard of? The concepts just don't match up. The Church has adapted before and will do so again – and again – and yet we must remember our roots, our purpose, the different kingdom to which we belong:

We have heard a summons to a kingdom that lies ahead. The future is what defines us. We must not be trapped by nostalgia, not defined by the present 'crisis'. Unless we want to resign ourselves to being rabbits in the headlights of a rushing juggernaut, we have to interrogate the assumptions we are forming.[9]

The Church is using the language of leadership now and there is no getting away from it. I am not with those who say that 'leadership is not a biblical world'. Or those who hold that the world of the Church and the world of 'glass and steel towers and corporate headquarters'[10] are completely separate things, with nothing to learn from one another. While we're at it, 'priest' is not a biblical word either when used to refer to one person – other than Christ – but that doesn't seem to stop some sections of the Church using it a great deal. Both 'priesthood' and 'leadership' are certainly seen throughout the Bible, in different forms, even if the nouns are rarely used in the same way that we use them today. There's plenty of leadership in the Bible, even if it doesn't have that name. But if we are thinking about what it means to lead in the image of the Father, and with the authority of our status as (albeit premature) ambassadors of his kingdom, then we need to become very adept at discernment. We need wisdom, and the finely tuned eyes and ears of the Spirit of God to help us to see what should be welcomed as for the Church and what should be rejected as coming from a 'lesser kingdom'. Baptist pastor Ian Stackhouse writes:

> To minister in Christ's name is to abandon the pristine world of success-driven suburbia, and instead to discern the contours of grace in the most unlikely people; it is to jettison the controlled, and often cliché ridden world of performance related work, and instead to take risks; and finally, lest ministry is reduced to nothing more than

a series of truisms, ministering in Christ's name is to relinquish the need for recognition, and embrace instead the obscurity of the cross.[11]

It is to the cross we now turn.

Cross-shaped leadership: success and failure with the grace of the Son

Weber's category of rational-legal authority refers to the right to lead that comes from election, rules, policies, bureaucracy. It is based on winning elections, earning promotion, demonstrating competency. In our society, leadership must be successful. Football managers are quickly sacked if they fail to win trophies, politicians anxiously watch their poll ratings, leaders are judged on their statistics and rapidly deposed when they dip. But, as we have seen, success in Christian leadership will look very different from that in business or politics or football.

Jesus was arguably the most successful person who ever lived, yet he lived a short life that ended in apparent ignominy on a cross, or so his aggressors supposed, whose followers deserted him, yet whose 'failure' was nevertheless the foundation stone of God's mission in the world. The hymn written by the earliest Church about this is found in Philippians 2.5–11 and it is the very best model for ambitious leaders who seek to follow his example:

> Let the same mind be in you that was in Christ Jesus,
> who, though he was in the form of God,

did not regard equality with God
  as something to be exploited,
but emptied himself,
  taking the form of a slave,
  being born in human likeness.
And being found in human form,
  he humbled himself
  and became obedient to the point of death –
  even death on a cross.
Therefore God also highly exalted him
  and gave him the name
  that is above every name,
so that at the name of Jesus
  every knee should bend,
  in heaven and on earth and under the earth,
and every tongue should confess
  that Jesus Christ is Lord,
  to the glory of God the Father.

Bradbury calls this Jesus' journey of 'descendent ambition.'[12] In line with all the other 'great reversals' of Jesus' ministry, 'The proclamation of the cross replaces an emphasis on achieving with an opposing emphasis on receiving.'[13] Of course, we will not, should not, cannot ever imagine that we could copy, or ever come close to, what Jesus achieved on the cross. He was God incarnate and we are certainly not. As Bonhoeffer writes in his astounding piece on the 'failure' of the cross, neither the 'success' nor the 'failure' of Christ is something we should consider it possible to emulate:

It is then precisely the cross of Christ, and thus precisely the failure Christ incurs in the world that again leads to historic success is a mystery of divine governance from which no "rule" be derived but which does repeat itself here and there in the suffering of his community.[14]

Nevertheless, the self-emptying of Jesus on the cross provides a corrective to all our temptations to get carried away with success and achievement based on strength, capability and power. The cross reframes entirely what we think of as constituting success at all. It can be so easy to become obsessed with observable success as a leader (much as we mutter things about not being concerned with that sort of thing), and to forget that, to outside eyes, the ministry of Jesus looked anything but successful. Or effective. There is a good deal of performance anxiety around in the Church at the moment and it can be very easy to get caught up in its stresses. The answer is neither to hanker after success, nor to embrace failure (or 'pain, lowliness, failure, poverty, loneliness, despair'[15]) as being inevitable or as having value in and of themselves.

As Christian leaders, we stand in the paradox of successful failure. There is a conundrum here. Christian leaders, priests in particular, will always be those who stand in the gap between what is and what should be, and bring one to the other. Whenever a priest hears the sins of the people, yet proclaims the forgiveness of God, whenever a leader takes on themselves the pain of their community, yet still stands, whenever a leader sees great numerical or financial success in their organization, yet remains truly humble, they come close to the 'special dark privilege'[16] of leadership in the image of the self-emptying Son:

> It is the intersection of tragedy and hope that makes the shape of the cross visible in ministry. Ministry whose excellence can be measured by the breadth and length and height and depth of God's love combines a vulnerability to human tragedy and a deep and persistent hope that enables resistance to evil and celebration of grace and new life.[17]

There is sin, but there is forgiveness. There is pain, but there is hope. There is failure, but there is success. I knew one church leader who, after a particular turbulent period in the life of his church, asked the congregation to spend some time one Sunday morning writing down on a timeline all the difficult, painful, joyful and significant events in the life of that community over the preceding five years. There had been illness, untimely deaths, divorce, but also marriages, births, conversions, ordinations and growth. At the end of the time, the leader simply stood at the front of the church and read out what was written on the paper he held. The weight of representing the rich life of that community, with all its successes and failures, broke his heart and he wept before the congregation. That was the priestly thing to do.

As we watch other leaders in the city, our politicians, celebrities, leaders of big business, being held up and cast down according to the whims and vagaries of popular opinion, according to how successful or otherwise they are, we need to be sure to base our authority on our calling and qualification by Christ, and on the knowledge that our ability to do anything comes from his strength rather than our own. When Paul analysed the success of his ministry towards the end of his life, he was able to say only, 'I have fought the good fight, I have finished the race, I have kept the faith' (2 Timothy 4.7).

Community-shaped leadership: vision and charisma in the fellowship of the Holy Spirit

Weber's charismatic authority category describes the, 'exceptional sanctity, heroism, or exemplary character'[18] of the leader. It all depends on the personal appeal of the individual. Politicians and celebrities rely on a sense of personal charisma to uphold their authority to lead, and when it is either overdone, or lacking, it is noticed and commented on. Where charisma waxes and wanes, authority is lost, and fast. For Christian leaders, 'charisma' takes on a very different meaning, of course. 'Charisma' relates, rather, to the grace gifts of the Holy Spirit of God (*charismata* is the word the New Testament uses for the gifts or graces of the Holy Spirit). As Christian leaders, we rely not on our own personal va-va-voom, but on the gifts and empowering of the Holy Spirit, who breathes life into our endeavours.

The Holy Spirit is the one who points forward to that wonderful day when the kingdom of God will be fully established on earth and, in signs and wonders, gives us a glimpse of that future-orientated kingdom. The Holy Spirit is given to us as a down payment, a promise, a guarantee, a sign of the future reality of that coming kingdom. As Paul puts it in his letter to the Ephesians:

> In him you also, when you had heard the word of truth, the gospel of your salvation, and had believed in him, were marked with the seal of the promised Holy Spirit; this is the pledge of our inheritance towards redemption as God's own people, to the praise of his glory.
> (Ephesians 1.13–14)

And again in 2 Corinthians, 'But it is God who establishes us with you in Christ and has anointed us, by putting his seal on us and giving us his Spirit in our hearts as a first instalment' (2 Corinthians 1.21). Ray Anderson puts it like this: 'The Spirit comes that comes to the church comes out of the future, not the past.'[19]

One of the tasks of Christian leadership is to constantly hold before our churches and communities, through the gifts, fruits and power of the Holy Spirit, that hope-filled future heralded by the Spirit of God, even if the reality of the present looks anything but hopeful. As truly 'charismatic' leaders, we stand in the gap between the now and the not-yet of the kingdom. We are acutely aware of the pain and we see success through the lens of the cross – yet we also dare to believe in resurrection and hope for that day when God's kingdom will be fully realized, and every tear will be wiped from every eye and the dwelling of God will be with mortals, and all will be well on earth. A little boy I know who is dairy-intolerant summed this yearning for the future in the fully realized kingdom when he went to a birthday party, at the end of which he exclaimed with great passion, 'In heaven, God will take all the dairy out of all the cakes!' Another friend, who suffers from chronic back pain sighed as she said, 'Heaven will have no stairs.' We feel the pain of the present, yet we know there is a better future coming (and we can work towards it ourselves also, making dairy-free cakes and helping our buildings to be accessible).

Therefore, while we may not rely on our own personal charisma to do so, we do need to be people who inspire others in winsome ways to aim high for the greater future God has promised, holding out a vision of hope: 'Leaders of institutions need to be able to see what is as well as what might be.'[20] Hope is a valuable commodity and, if nothing else, a leader must be a 'dealer in hope',[21] all the while keeping in view the realties of this present age.

When the England football team progressed further than they had done for a while in the World Cup of 2017, I saw hope against hope in the faces of my husband and son as their team prevailed through a penalty shoot-out to reach the quarter finals. Could this be the year that football would finally come home? Could it possibly be? Could it . . .? They kind of knew it wouldn't be, of course, somewhere deep down, yet they, and the rest of the nation with them, hoped like mad, held together by an honest appraisal of the likelihood of that happening. Holding in tension the hope and the reality is the task of the leader.

Trinity College has seen an increase in student numbers over the past couple of years. I think it might be because we stopped focusing on the difficulties and challenges facing the Church of England (although our students are equipped to face the present realities) and began to speak more about a vision of the future, expressed in our theologically interesting and grammatically slightly incorrect strapline 'Live like the kingdom is near.' We spoke at open days and interviews, not about the latest Church divisions and the challenges of the parish system, but about the need for our students to be citizens of the kingdom, declaring the realities of the coming kingdom wherever they see them.

We constantly asked ourselves: What would it look like if we truly *lived like the kingdom was near*? What if we really took seriously Jesus call to seek first God's kingdom? If the kingdom is here already but not yet fully, how might living further towards the 'not-yet' influence all we say and do, and teach and learn and practise in ministry? I don't think there will be theological colleges in the fully realized kingdom (but you never know), but if there were, what would one look like? What would they teach? There won't be meetings in heaven (I hope), but if there were, what would they be like? And so we allowed God's future to shape and mould the way we live in the present. When we live in the light of the eternity of the coming kingdom, we will see the present task of theological education as training ministers, who become more and more 'kingdom-like' in the way they learn, lead and live. Time and again when we have later surveyed students who have accepted a place to train with us, the box most frequently ticked in response to the question 'Why did you choose Trinity?' was 'Vision'.

There is a great deal of pressure on leaders today to fit their businesses, organizations, churches for the challenges of the future. But for the Christian leader, we have a further, longer, higher, deeper vision than simply the future. The future is uncertain and unknown. C. S. Lewis in *The Screwtape Letters* says that there are four periods: past, present, future and eternity. The devils, says Screwtape to his nephew, Wormwood, wish to lead people away from God by getting them to focus either on the past or on the future. The perils of focusing on the past are clear, but the perils of focusing too much on the future are equally stark:

> Thought about the Future inflames hope and fear. Also, it is unknown to them, so that in making them think about it we make them think of unrealities. In a word, the Future is, of all things, the thing least like eternity.[22]

God, he says, wants his followers 'to attend chiefly to two things, to eternity itself, and to that point of time which they call the Present. For the Present is the point at which time touches eternity'.[23] The Welsh poet R. S. Thomas paints a similar picture in his poem 'The bright field':

> Life is not hurrying / on to a receding future, nor hankering after / an imagined past. It is the turning / aside like Moses to the miracle / of the lit bush, to a brightness / that seemed as transitory as your youth / once, but is the eternity that awaits you.[24]

We might call this 'living eschatologically'. It is what Jesus did by talking about his kingdom. He drew his followers' attention not towards the future, which was uncertain, but towards eternity, which was clear, starting from the present. He began his earthly ministry with the words, 'The time is fulfilled, and the kingdom of God has come near; repent, and believe in the good news' (Mark 1.15). And he went round showing and talking about his kingdom, with its fulfilment in eternity, by pointing out the things of the present, saying, 'This is what the kingdom of heaven is like . . .'. N. T. Wright points out that when Jesus tried to do this kind of 'formation for eternity' with his disciples, it didn't always go well:

> Jesus announces the kingdom and summons his followers to share in the work of announcing and inaugurating it. Yet the kingdom confounds their expectations; they don't understand what's going on, and they fail to pick up the significance of his strange stories and powerful deeds. The story of the 'foundation of the church' in the Gospels does not show Jesus' first followers latching right on to his message and meaning and being sensibly and easily 'trained' to follow Jesus in putting the kingdom into effect.[25]

That's why Jesus told so many stories and parables and painted word pictures, forming and training his disciples to desire the kingdom increasingly in word and deed.

Being able to hear, gather, discern and reflect back the God-inspired vision for the future of a community is one of the most important skills of leadership. Jones calls this 'Learning to attend to God's beauty and to see and hear through God-inspired eyes and ears'.[26] As such, we will need leaders with imagination, leaders who are able to see the things of this world, with all of its mess and difficulty, with eyes that are fixed on the beauty of eternity, 'We need pastors who can nurture congregations in imaginative reasoning through preaching and teaching, providing wise counsel and spiritual direction, and faithful and imaginative leadership and governance.'[27] Dykstra describes this kind of leadership like this:

> Such ministry has about it a freshness, an improvisatory character, a liveliness that is itself infectious. And thus an imagination that is at its heart a 'seeing in depth' turns out to be an imagination full of creativity – an imagination that sees what is not yet and begins to create it.[28]

I am aware that I am very much a 'glass half full' person, and not everyone is, but it seems to me that there will always be two ways of seeing the world: with hope or with despair. I heard a talk by the head teacher of a school in a deprived area of Bristol that had received an 'outstanding' rating by Ofsted. The school exists in a very tough context where it would be all too easy to focus on the challenges and difficulties. She listed a range of goals and values that her school held – academic excellence and personal development were up there – but right at the heart of her presentation was the word 'hope'. She saw the purpose of the school as to hold out hope to its students. Despite all the very real problems that surrounded the school and its pupils, they had chosen to focus on hope.

We can choose, in the way we present reality, to focus on the positive or the negative. Jonathan Sacks examines God's call to Moses and the people of God in Deuteronomy 30, framed as a choice between life and death, blessings and curses, to follow God or to follow the gods of neighbouring lands: 'Choose life, that you and your children may live.'[29] Sacks says that it is the task of the leader to define reality by interpreting the meaning of events for the people: 'How we interpret the world affects how we respond to the world, and it is our responses that shape our lives, individually and collectively.'[30] A story is told in 2 Kings 6.15–17 of when the king of Aram sent troops to Dothan to encircle the prophet Elisha. When Elisha's servant saw that they were surrounded, he panicked. But Elisha prayed, 'O LORD, please open his eyes that he might see!' and the servant's vision was enlarged, to see that they were, in fact, surrounded by horses and chariots, troops on their side. The reality of the vision was quite different from how the situation first appeared, but it took the eyes of faith to see it. To see with God's eternal eyes and to hold out that hope to our communities will take great strength. Not the strength that comes from having a huge, personal charisma, but the strength that comes from having all the resources and gifts of the Holy Spirit at our disposal. For us, charismatic leadership must be understood, not as the cult of personality, but as having an infilling and empowering with the gifts of the Holy Spirit given to the whole Church for strengthening and building up the body of Christ.

One of the things all leaders can bring to their task is enthusiasm. People need to see a bit of life, a bit of verve, a bit of passion (yes, even Anglicans). The root of the word 'enthusiasm' is in the Greek, *en* – in, *theos* – God, and means, literally, divine inspiration or infilling. Some of the earliest charismatic movements were called 'Enthusiasts' because of their fervour and their Spirit-inspired worship. Some leaders are very serious and gloomy. Perhaps we need again to recover this sense of holy cheerfulness, inspired by the hope-filled visions of eternity held out to us by God's indwelling Spirit.

There are a couple of further things to say about vision. First, discerning vision is never a solo activity. This is not about the Big Leader ascending the mountain to bring down the word from God on stone tablets to the followers waiting eagerly below. Discerning hope-filled vision for the future in the light of eternity is the task of the whole Christian community. When I took up my post at Trinity College, I spent the first six months listening to the hopes, dreams and visions of different groups within the college community – students, staff, trustees and the families of students. From that time of discussing, listening and praying emerged the vision to 'Live like the kingdom is near.' The task of the leader is to gather all that they are hearing from God, within the community, and to distil and reflect it back in a way that can be grasped and understood. Discerning vision is something that must be done in community, with the fellowship of the Holy Spirit. So, 'Visionary leaders involve the whole community in the Christian practice of discernment, helping them imagine possibilities and then take faithful risks that they might otherwise be unwilling to take.'[31] We preside within, not above, the life of the community, winsomely holding out the hope of God's future, any charisma we have coming from the gifting and empowering of the Holy Spirit, who gives gifts to the whole body of Christ.

Second, having vision should not be at the expense of having common sense. Beware the 'wishfulness of big dreams'. We can choose to be either disappointed idealists or optimistic realists.[32] Visions need to be acted upon and to be helped to become reality, with a sense of time, using available resources, planning next steps, communicating with clarity and checking progress. It is no good having a dream if the practical strategy to achieve that dream is completely out of reach. There is a need for a sense of realism in vision-casting, and timescales are important. Our horizon may be eternity, but what will we do next Tuesday?

A *Harvard Business Review* article by Herminia Ibarra and Otilia Obodaru cites a study showing that women leaders often score better than their male peers in several leadership dimensions, except one: envisioning. Their contention is that women leaders come to more senior leadership posts with 'a strong command of the technical elements of their jobs and a nose to the grindstone focus on accomplishing quantifiable objectives', but that they then need also to allow the leadership skill of 'crafting and articulating a vision of a better future'[33] to come to the fore as they step into roles in which realizing change becomes a central expectation. If a leader, male or female, is able to bring together the hard graft of leading with and through the practical realities, developing strategies and communicating well, along with the ability to hold out winsome and compelling visions of future possibilities, or at least to encourage these things both to happen through others, then the whole community will benefit: '[Vision] encompasses the abilities to frame the current practices as inadequate, to generate ideas for new strategies, and to communicate possibilities in inspiring ways to others.'[34] Ibarra and Obodaru coin the term, 'practical futurists' for what is required.

Ambitious leaders who aim to offer servant leadership according to the patterns of the kingdom of God will recognize that their authority is set in a context that is different from that sometimes seen around them: an authority that is creator-shaped, cross-shaped and community-shaped, following the image of Father, Son and Holy Spirit. We exist as premature ambassadors, confidently representing our King, resisting the temptation to accept the power of a lesser authority, despite the awkwardness. We determine to stand in the cross-shaped gap and mediate between what is and what could be, which enables us to see success and effectiveness through very different lenses. And we preside within the life of the community, winsomely holding out the hope of God's future, any charisma we have coming from the gifting and empowering of the Holy Spirit. In order to offer this kind of leadership, we will need anchor points, ways of thinking about ourselves and our contexts, ways that keep us close to the ethos of kingdom. Jesus held out a vision for what it looks like to be a citizen of his kingdom when he went up the mountain, sat down and began to speak and taught them, saying . . .

6

Key spiritual dispositions for ambitious people

When Jesus saw the crowds, he went up the mountain; and after he sat down, his disciples came to him. Then he began to speak, and taught them, saying:
'Blessed are the poor in spirit, for theirs is the kingdom of heaven.
'Blessed are those who mourn, for they will be comforted.
'Blessed are the meek, for they will inherit the earth.
'Blessed are those who hunger and thirst for righteousness, for they will be filled.
'Blessed are the merciful, for they will receive mercy.
'Blessed are the pure in heart, for they will see God.
'Blessed are the peacemakers, for they will be called children of God.
'Blessed are those who are persecuted for righteousness' sake, for theirs is the kingdom of heaven.'
(Matthew 5.1–10, The Beatitudes)

Blessed . . .

When Jesus went up the mountain, sat down and told his followers what it looks like to be a citizen of the kingdom of God, he used a certain word over and over again. Blessed.

In Greek, *makarios*. Bible translators have struggled with knowing how best to render the word. 'Blessed' is most commonly used, but isn't quite there. It sounds too conditional, too passive ('do this and God will bless you'). Some have tried 'happy', but that's not quite right either. Tom Wright goes with, 'Wonderful news for . . .'[1] Dick France suggests, 'Good on ya!'[2] Scot McKnight claims that 'on this word the entire passage stands, and from this one word the whole list hangs. Get this word right, the rest falls into place; get it wrong, and the whole thing falls apart.'[3]

To link what Jesus is saying here with the grand narrative of Scripture, seeing Jesus as the fulfilment of the law and the prophets, we note the allusion to Moses delivering the ten commandments from the mountainside. In this light, proclaiming 'blessedness' stands in the Old Testament tradition of speaking about human flourishing, which, arguably, is a much richer description than the rather bland 'blessed' suggests.[4] *Makarios* is a highly formulaic word, included in a recognizable structure that reflects the Hebrew form, *asre*, found, for example, in Psalm 1.1: 'Happy are those who do not follow the advice of the wicked.' It is a fulsome description of human flourishing in every respect, fullness of life, well-being, the good life, peace with God, self, neighbour and creation, the sweet-spot, life in abundance – *shalom*. Jesus holds out a vision for human flourishing that is inspirational. This is what it looks like to live well in God's creation, with God, with fellow human beings, within oneself and with the whole created order. Therefore:

This is not a 'grin and bear it' approach to simply 'keep calm and carry on' in the midst of difficulties, but an invitation to rejoice due to the realization that this state is true human flourishing now and in the age to come.[5]

How *not* to read the Beatitudes

There is a right and a wrong way to read the Beatitudes. The key is in that word *makarios*. It does not mean 'the one whom God blesses'. The Greek word for that would be *eulogetos*. *Makarios* describes a way of being, a condition of life, a state of blessedness *that already exists*, rather than something that will happen to you if you do a certain thing. The construction is not, 'If you are poor in spirit and so on, then God will bless you.' It is, 'If you find yourself poor in spirit, you are, despite appearances, blessed if you are a citizen of the kingdom, because of God's future promises, begun in the present.' Wright says that the Beatitudes are 'a summons to live in the present in a way that will make sense in God's promised future, because that future has arrived in the present in Jesus of Nazareth.'[6]

Therefore, the Beatitudes are not instructions to try ever so hard at something, like New Year's resolutions or Dry January; 'They do not indicate conditions that are especially pleasing to God or good for human beings.'[7] These sayings are more descriptive than prescriptive. If you find yourself being in this, or that, state, then consider yourself blessed if you count yourself as a citizen of the kingdom.

I originally intended to title this chapter, 'Key spiritual *disciplines* for ambitious people', but that would have been to miss the point. These are not disciplines to be kept in order to please God or earn his blessing, or even to live life better. They are descriptions of people who are already in his kingdom and, therefore, find themselves blessed or happy. They are people who are 'blessed', not 'blest'. A better title for them might be The Felicitudes: The Fortunate Ones.

Having said all that, it is not unreasonable to say that vision and practices inform and influence each other. Given that the people to whom Jesus addresses his teaching were considered to be blessed in the kingdom, it is perhaps not completely out of the question to suggest that we might consider what would it look like for us today to be blessed in the same way, whether or not we are poor in spirit, persecuted, hungry and thirsty for righteousness and so on. Jesus wasn't talking directly to us when he said blessed are the meek, but to his disciples and (arguably) those others in the crowd listening in, all a rather rag-tag bunch, people oppressed by a foreign regime and living under the misapprehension that if you were poor or sick or downtrodden it was because of something you (or your parents) had done. We are not they. Yet, in observing what Jesus said to them about their place in his kingdom, we have much to learn and, quite possibly, emulate in our own lives and leadership. As Pennington says, 'One misreads the Beatitudes if they are taken as mere statements of God's blessing without recognizing that inherent in a macarism is an appeal to live a certain way that will result in our flourishing',[8] not least because these statements also precisely describe the life of Jesus Christ, our model and our example for good living, the humble, mourning, merciful, pure, peace-bringing, suffering servant.

There is, in what Jesus says, an essence of what the kingdom looks like that is aspirational and inspirational for ambitious people. They describe the character of the kingdom and, if we seek to be citizens of this kingdom, we might aim for our character to be in line with this description. The Beatitudes, therefore, offer us a helpful check to the potential excesses of ambition and, precisely because the kingdom of God is so radically different from the kingdoms of this world, provide us with a way of assessing our behaviours, choices, aspirations and habits in the light of God's values and characteristics.

So perhaps *disciplines* is not the right word. Neither, really, is *practices*. So I have settled for *dispositions* and hope you will be content with that. They are, at the very least, an important pair of spectacles through which to view our attitudes. As we saw in Chapter 3 we are people who desire our way around the world. And the way we train our desires to be orientated towards the kingdom is through daily habits that shape our dispositions to desire kingdom ways. As Smith puts it, 'Faithful, dynamic practices and habits beget others, practice unfolding into practice as we live into our lives together.'[9] So the question is, how do we live in such a way as to enable the 'faithful, dynamic practices' that arise from the states personified in the Beatitudes to train our dispositions, and hence desires, for the things of the kingdom, and how do we allow that to influence who we are as leaders, in whatever context we find ourselves?

My hunch is that you and I wouldn't even start where Jesus does, if it were up to us. In natural human ways, these descriptions of blessedness would be peculiar things to aim for. The blessed ones are those who are poor in spirit, those who mourn, the meek, the hungry and thirsty for righteousness, the merciful, the pure in heart, the peacemakers and the persecuted. You wouldn't find a list like this in any lifestyle magazine suggesting ways of good living: ten simple steps to becoming poorer in spirit! Hints and tips for the merciful! Five great ways to be persecuted! (and a delicious recipe for flapjack). William Willimon writing about the apparent foolishness of the Beatitudes says:

> Try being meek tomorrow at work and see how far you get. Meekness is fine for church, but in the real world the meek get to go home early with a pat on the back. Blessed are those who are peacemakers; they shall get done to them what they are loath to do to others. Blessed are the merciful; they shall get it done to them a second time. Blessed are those who are persecuted for righteousness' sake; they shall be called fanatics.[10]

These are indeed strange things to connect with blessedness and flourishing. But they describe those who live according to the alternative realities of God's kingdom.

So let's see how living according to this rather strange-looking set of descriptions or commitments might help us in our living and leading in some of the areas we have been examining in this book – ambition, counting, strategy, comparisons, authority, success, vision.

The Beatitudes for ambitious leaders

1 Stay (properly) humble

> Blessed are the poor in spirit, for theirs is the kingdom of Heaven.

In Luke's version of the Beatitudes the 'in spirit' bit drops off and it is specifically the materially poor who are blessed, with a corresponding woe for the rich. But 'poor in spirit' here in Matthew seems to move away from being about material wealth alone and includes both poor and (potentially) rich, and *all who regard themselves as utterly dependent on God.* That is the essence of what it means to be poor in spirit. The word in Greek literally means 'the bent low ones'. For those of us who consider ourselves ambitious, this is an excellent place to start. Humility is not the opposite of ambition, it is a central component of it:

> Humility is the foundation of any genuine spirituality for it concerns the ground of our being. It doesn't mean feeling wretched about ourselves but realising the truth of who we are in the eyes of God; that we are dust, but dust destined for glory' (Eph. 3. 3.14ff.).[11]

Having a drive for excellence and a desire to see things change can go hand in hand with a humble attitude.

But only if it is *real* humility. Not humility in a Uriah Heap ever so 'umble kind of way. Not humility in the sense of Donald Trump who boasted: 'I think I am, actually humble. I think I'm much more humble than you would understand.'[12] If you think you're humble, you're probably not. If you try to be humble, you probably can't. Tim Keller says, 'Humility is so shy. If you begin talking about it, it leaves.'[13] It is said that Gregory the Great resisted elevation to the papacy precisely because he feared the temptation brought by its associated power to present supposed humility as a cover for actual pride.[14] If we paint humility as a kind of virtue, as something you have to try harder to get better at, we will miss entirely what is meant by this first Beatitude or any of the rest of them for that matter. It could be very easy for the ambitious to try and outdo each other at being humble. We'd never admit to it, of course, because that wouldn't look very humble, but there could be the temptation to have a kind of humbler-than-thou competition.

To be 'poor in spirit' means something a lot less appealing than the gloss we might be inclined to put on it. Poor in spirit would not have had positive overtones for Jesus' listeners at all. They wouldn't have thought 'gracefully and positively humble', as we tend to think, but, rather, spiritually destitute, bent over, helplessly trusting in God because they have to, even though it gets them nowhere with anyone. It refers to those who are nowhere in terms of status or influence or even, religiously speaking, those who are not considered spiritually rich by anyone's standards, even their own, those who don't know the answers, who don't have any titles, who are not sure even where they stand with the systems of the day, those who know deep down that it is through God's grace only that they can ever stand at all. If we substitute 'poor in spirit' with 'spiritual poverty', it takes on a very different feel. This is about a poverty of pride, a real, almost desperate, dependence on God for everything. Translations that speak of 'spiritual helplessness' or 'destitution' or 'bankruptcy' probably come closer to the mark.

These are the ones whom Jesus calls 'blessed'.

Jane Williams says that such people are at somewhat of an advantage in apprehending the 'merciful humility' of God, because:

those who never had any illusions about their own abilities find it easier to accept the merciful humility of God, that notices them, makes space for them, draws them in as valued parts of the human story of being called into relationship with God.[15]

This is a stark reminder for those of us who are ambitious, who like to see things grow and change, who want to be the best that we can be. All of it must always be dependent wholly on God, his grace and his provision, rather than our own efforts, however hard we might try. As someone who has risen pretty well to what life throws at me, someone who Copes, an Enneagram number 3, the temptation is always to believe that I can do this thing – life, ministry, leadership, whatever – in my own strength. Becoming humble is increasingly submitting myself to God's kingship, power and providence in complete and total dependence on him. It is turning away from the attitude that says 'I know best', 'I'm in charge of my life', 'I am quite competent and capable of managing on my own thanks very much', 'I've got this', towards the knowledge that it is God's work, God's Church, God's kingdom; the truth that will sustain me is the fact that God works in and through me, rather than it being anything I do in my own strength.

Graham Tomlin rightly suggests that leadership in the kingdom of God must be all about humility:

Any personal ambition, any longing for reputation, praise or self-focused glory will inevitably lead attention away from the true leader of the church, Jesus Christ, and place it on the leader him or herself. Now of course this is a counsel of perfection. It is impossible to purge oneself entirely of ambition and traces of self worship, yet to the extent that they are present in the life of a priest or Christian leader, they will undermine and corrupt the distinctively Christian character of the leadership that is offered.[16]

Admitting limitations to our own capacity for action is not only an essential spiritual discipline, but also (wouldn't you know) an effective leadership tool. In his seminal work on why some businesses succeed where others don't, Jim Collins found that the qualities exhibited by those who led successful organizations were 'a fierce personal resolve' combined 'with a deep personal humility'.[17] Good leaders exhibit the passion to see the job done, coupled with humility to admit that they don't know all the answers. Edmondson, in her book on encouraging psychological safety in the workplace, points to the need for the leader to 'Be a don't knower'. In other words, to admit they don't know everything and therefore to engage in what she calls 'humble listening'.[18] J. K. Rowling identified three essential qualities for being a successful author: resilience, courage and humility.[19] So, although Jesus was referring to a distinctive dependence on God when he spoke of those who are poor in spirit, it appears that humility is also an effective leadership disposition.

For the past six years, I have led pre-ordination retreats for those about to be ordained as deacons or priests in the Church of England. It is an immense privilege, and I have loved journeying with people at this crucial point in their lives, as all the years of searching, discernment and training come to a head and they submit themselves in grateful service to the one who has called and sustained them. There are more than a few nerves. It doesn't help (or maybe it does) that the whole thing is usually silent, so people have plenty of time alone with their thoughts and musings. Part of the role of the retreat leader is to make oneself available to speak individually with those preparing for ordination. One after the other, without fail, they come and say, 'I'm not sure I can do this.' To which I say, 'No, you're absolutely right. Well done. You have just discovered the key to successful ministry.' You *can't* do it. But God can.

One of my abiding memories is of my own ordination as deacon in Sheffield Cathedral. As part of that service, we ordinands were required, while the *Veni Creator* was being sung, to prostrate ourselves, lying face down on the cold, hard stone floor of the cathedral. For some considerable time. I was pregnant at the time so it was something of a logistical challenge, and one aspect of my memory is of fighting the urge to puke. Not a good look for an ordinand. But what that posture taught me then, and reminds me now, is that only in laying down our own rights, claims and abilities in complete and utter dependence on the empowering and filling of his Holy Spirit will any kind of ministry be possible.

What goes for individuals goes also for us as a Church. If we are to seek audacious goals, we must be what Bonhoeffer would call 'the fellowship of the undevout', together truly knowing our need of God and his grace and forgiveness daily. If by humility we mean fostering a poverty of spirit that recognizes our absolute need for God's grace to be able to exist at all in the face of our guilt and failure and helplessness and emptiness – and a deep hunger for the work of his Holy Spirit to do anything – then perhaps we come closer to what this Beatitude means. Contrary to appearances, this is good news! This is an invitation to, and a vision for, wonderful flourishing in the light of the coming kingdom. It is an invitation to rejoice, because those who follow Christ in poverty of spirit are inheritors of his kingdom. Jane Williams points to the power of humility, not least because in humility we reflect the very nature of God

> We are sent out to practise merciful humility, as sisters and brothers of the Son. God stoops to make the earth home, the Son 'empties himself' to fill us with life. There is no place where God cannot be found, peacefully working an unimaginable future, with the humble and merciful power of resurrection life.[20]

2 Seek wholeness (but not necessarily only your own)

Blessed are those who mourn, for they will be comforted.

With all that has been said about ambition and the drive for success, it seems that the main need is to keep a check on motivation. What am I doing all this for? Is it for my own advancement and fame or to fulfil the calling God has placed on my life to join with him in ushering in his kingdom in the world?

This is where this second Beatitude comes in. Blessed are those who mourn. Mourn what? This verse has, perhaps not entirely wrongly, been seen and used as a means of comfort for those going through bereavement, the loss of a loved one. But set in the wider context of the story of the Messiah who speaks these words of blessedness, it takes on another, additional, meaning.[21] The word for 'those who mourn' is *penthountes*. In other places in the Gospels, this is the word that is used for those who mourn and wait for the bridegroom, the image used for the coming Christ, the Messiah who will set all things right in his kingdom. This is mourning the current reality in the light of what could be, and what is to come. It is mourning that has a future focus.

The Beatitudes clearly reflect some of the same themes as Isaiah 61.1–4, part of which is quoted by Jesus as a kind of 'mission statement' for the whole of his ministry:

> The Spirit of the LORD is upon me,
>   because he has anointed me
>   to bring good news to the poor.
> He has sent me to proclaim release to the captives
>   and recovery of sight to the blind,
>   to let the oppressed go free,
> to proclaim the year of the LORD's favour.
> (Luke 4.18–19)

The particular focus for the comforting in Isaiah is 'to provide for those who mourn in Zion', those who mourn the destruction of Jerusalem and who long to see a restoration both of the city and of justice for its people. It is a cry against oppression and poverty and a yearning for the comfort of the wholeness and shalom of the coming kingdom of the Messiah for all.

This is a good vision for the ambitious – to set all our efforts within the framework of a holy dissatisfaction that longs for a coming of God's kingdom. To live in the light of this Beatitude may mean a similar cry for the kingdom of God to be seen more fully in your area of influence or ministry, working to see that more of a reality than it would have otherwise been without your presence and gifts. What is it that causes you to mourn in your context? For more people in your community to know the healing and restoring comfort of Christ? His wholeness? For your school to be the kind of place where children are enabled to flourish in all aspects of life, not only academic achievement? Allow that sense of grief for 'what is not yet, but could be' to be a motivation for your leadership and hear in the process the proclamation of 'comfort by God' for those who seek the ways of his kingdom and choose to follow the King.

If we are going to talk about growth and success, as we should, this Beatitude reminds us that unless we keep the vision of kingdom of God at front and centre of all we do – wholeness, shalom, not just for ourselves, but for those most badly affected by the current state of the world – we will miss the mark. This might not be short-term comfort. We may never see the full fruits of our labours on earth, but we allow this sense of holy dissatisfaction with what is, in light of what could be, to drive our ambitions for change.

3 Show (gentle) compassion

Blessed are the meek, for they will inherit the earth.

There is some debate about whether 'meek' speaks of those who are humble and gentle or of those who are materially poor. Both would make sense in the light of the promise that such people will 'inherit the earth'. Meekness is not weakness but, rather, gentleness of the quality described in Colossians 3.12, 'As God's chosen ones, holy and beloved, clothe yourselves with compassion, kindness, humility, *meekness*, and patience' (my emphasis). Remember that Jesus describes such people as blessed in the context of his here and coming kingdom. Kingdom. A word usually associated with rule, monarchy, kings, power, privilege, but in Christ subverted to mean something entirely different. Kingdoms are usually won in battle, with strategy and strong will. But this is the peaceable kingdom of the King of Peace.

The people of this kingdom are the 'powerless ones',[22] who will inherit the earth only through the death, resurrection and return of Christ and who will then fully establish his kingdom. In this we can have confidence, because 'the earth is the LORD's, and everything in it' (Psalm 24.1, NIV) and is therefore already the inheritance of the Lord's people. We are given the earth by Jesus – the one who, in the cross, has already secured it for himself.[23]

Those of us who like to plan, to strategize, to manoeuvre and engineer our way to success (whatever that looks like) do well to heed this call to meekness. In our driven, ambition-hungry world, there is not much room for meekness. One book on ambition (subtitled *Why it's good to want more and how to get it*) gives this advice, 'If you are serious about being successful, you need to make a commitment to yourself to see your goal through to its conclusion. And you need to invest your energies into making it happen.'[24] One of the pieces of advice on the way is 'Explain how you are different from all the other people with big ideas and why you will achieve your goal when others may not'.[25] This does not sound very much like meekness.

Embracing meekness does not mean that we eschew planning and strategizing. Being meek does not involve being wet or just hoping for the best. It is possessing a quiet, inner confidence that does not need to boast or assert itself over and above others – what Augustine describes as 'a certain firmness and stability of the perpetual inheritance'. He also says, 'Let those then who are not meek quarrel and fight for earthly and temporal things.'[26]

Meekness means refusing to join in with the power-hungry games of thrusting ambition – even for the sake of the gospel. I have known leaders who have an (initially) admirable drive and passion to achieve great things for Jesus, but who go about their mission with such disregard for the well-being of others that their goals are undone by the means by which they seek to achieve them. We can either spend our time anxiously battling to win the world for Christ or we can act with the deep, secure knowledge that the world already belongs to him, and that we – the meek – play our part in bringing that kingdom reality more into view by what we do and, more importantly, by the way we do it.

4 Pursue righteousness (by which we mean the holiness of God)

Blessed are those who hunger and thirst for righteousness, for they will be filled.

What is righteousness? In modern parlance, it has come to mean something like personal moral or ethical virtue – 'fulfil all righteousness', 'righteous anger'. So is this an injunction to try to be a better person, to be more successful at being an upright and ethical, to try just a little bit harder to be good? If so, then such hungering and thirsting after self-improvement is a common quest and a theme in popular literature and culture. Weekend newspaper supplements are full of articles on how to improve yourself in every imaginable way. Practise mindfulness, turn vegan, do more exercise. Is this just Jesus' take on self-improvement?

There is a better way of reading what Jesus says here, and that is to recognize the righteousness *of God* as the object of the hungering and thirsting (see, for example, Isaiah 51.1). The whole point is this is absolutely not a righteousness that can be earned by trying harder. Hungering and thirsting for righteousness is, rather, 'relationship with God focused on obedience.'[27] Pennington lands on a definition of righteousness in the Beatitudes, and in the whole Sermon on the Mount, as 'whole-person behavior that accords with God's nature, will, and kingdom'.[28] France calls it, 'A whole orientation of life towards God and his will'.[29] The key there is *whole* person. This kind of righteousness can never be skin deep but extends beyond mere actions to attitudes and inner heart orientation towards Christ. Elsewhere in Matthew, Jesus condemns the apparent righteousness of the Pharisees:

Woe to you, scribes and Pharisees, hypocrites! For you are like whitewashed tombs, which on the outside look

beautiful, but inside they are full of the bones of the dead and of all kinds of filth. So you also on the outside look righteous to others, but inside you are full of hypocrisy and lawlessness.
(Matthew 23.27)

And so this kind of righteousness, paradoxically, will be received as a grace-gift from God – not able to be earned, not a result of our being successful at anything. But such righteousness must also be wholeheartedly sought, thirsted after and hungered for, allowed to penetrate deep into character, disposition and habits, in a continual response to the free gift of grace given in Christ.

Even if the righteousness described is that imputed by God rather than earned by our hard works, which most scholars seem to recognize it is, the question remains, is this a righteousness to do with personal salvation or with God's wider work of 'setting the world to rights', which includes, inevitably, individual salvation from sin but also wider issues of justice, poverty and equality? Most likely it is both, with God's desire for justice within the whole cosmic order encompassing also individual repentance, turning from sin and a desire to find oneself within God's will. Thus, this is a 'yearning for the coming kingdom and the righteousness of God that will be realised in it: hungering for righteousness means a longing for the one who will bring justice to those suffering from violence.'[30]

What shape will this hunger and thirsting take for the Christian leader? This Beatitude speaks to that sense of desire that is so much part of the character of good leadership.

Leaders with godly ambition will be those who are passionate, dedicated, committed to the cause or community into which they have been called. The challenge of this Beatitude is to take that innate sense of passion and make sure it is focused in the right direction – towards the goodness of God and his work in the world to bring in his kingdom. It's a matter of perspective again. We are not to be those who place our own sense of self and personal ambition ahead of all else, but to be those who are prepared to submit our ambitions wholeheartedly to the will of Christ, saying, with Paul:

> I regard everything as loss because of the surpassing value of knowing Christ Jesus my Lord. For his sake I have suffered the loss of all things, and I regard them as rubbish, in order that I may gain Christ and be found in him, not having a righteousness of my own that comes from the law, but one that comes through faith in Christ, the righteousness from God based on faith.
> (Philippians 3.8–9)

5 Address inequality

Blessed are the merciful, for they will receive mercy.

Mercy is a prominent theme in the Sermon on the Mount and, indeed, throughout the Gospels. It usually involves compassion and forgiveness,[31] in the light of a God who is similarly merciful and forgiving (Exodus 34.6). It could imply those who release others from debts owed to them, either the debt of sin owed to God or other kinds of debt resulting from wrongdoing (see Matthew 18.23–25; 23.23; 6.12, 14–15; 9.13; 12.7). Just as we need to remember that righteousness involves not only actions but also heart response, so too we need to remember that mercy is not simply an attitude of heart, but also involves actions. Mercy is an 'effective disposition'. To be merciful is to commit to an action rather than simply be in a certain frame of mind.[32]

A common theme in the New Testament is God's preference for mercy over empty legalism or self-righteous judgement. Jesus twice quotes the prophet Hosea 'For I desire mercy, not sacrifice, and acknowledgment of God rather than burnt offerings' (Hosea 6.6, NIV), both in response to the reaction of the Pharisees. The first time is when they criticize him for eating at the house of the tax collector Matthew (once Levi); 'Go and learn what this means, "I desire mercy, not sacrifice." For I have come to call not the righteous but sinners' (Matthew 9.13). The second time is when they have a go at his disciples for plucking ears of grain on the Sabbath: 'But if you had known what this means, "I desire mercy and not sacrifice", you would not have condemned the guiltless' (Matthew 12.7).

The whole point of sacrifice is that it releases the one doing the sacrificing from the debt of the wrongdoing that they carry. The point about mercy is that it releases the debtor from needing to make a sacrifice at all. Hence the ultimate mercy is found in the action of Christ on the cross, releasing sinners from the debt of sin. Christ who was without sin became sin for us. This is the basis of mercy. When we show mercy, we give something up in order that someone else may gain something. Mercy is about true levelling, not unequal compassion. To show mercy to someone is to say, 'Look, you owe me something, but I will bear the burden of that instead.' Mercy is an act of extreme sharing and equality. It involves the powerful giving power to the weak. It means one person letting go of potential gain in order to release the debtor. Showing mercy brings the giver down to the place where the receiver is, so that mercy receivers are on a par with mercy-givers. Augustine highlights the reciprocal nature of mercy in this Beatitude: 'To the merciful, mercy, as to those following a true and excellent counsel, so that this same treatment is extended toward them by one who is stronger, which they extend towards the weaker.'[33]

How might we think about this in the context of ambition? Mercy is the great leveller. To show someone mercy is not to patronize them and look down on them; it is to say, 'Come up and stand where I am' or, possibly, 'Let me come down and stand where you are.' It makes a mockery of promotion, selfish ambition, hierarchy or the success of one person demanding the failure of another. It is doing things that may not benefit you or your career, but which might help someone else. It is not using people's mistakes to cause them to fear, but to enable them to learn and grow. It is promoting your neighbour's church website. It is Retweeting the Tweet of the leader of an organization that is your competitor. It is praising the successes of others with which you had nothing to do. It is giving away something that would have benefited your organization, so that another might grow.

And it is doing all that without anyone even sharing it on Facebook.

6 Spend time alone with God

Blessed are the pure in heart, for they will see God.

The blessedness of those who are pure in heart has a particular draw as we consider the potentially murky realms of ambition and success. How many of us would long to be truly 'pure in heart'? If we were pure in heart, surely all the rest of this – ambition, the approval monster, success, effectiveness, growth, power – would all take its rightful place?

The psalmist speaks of those who have clean hands and a pure heart (Psalm 24). These are the ones who can ascend the hill of the Lord. This is about inner motives (pure heart) matching external actions (clean hands) and there being integrity between the two. As with so many of the Beatitudes this is about inner and outer life being in alignment. In relation to ambition, this is a timely reminder to make sure that who we are in public is the same as who we are when no one is looking. If one is ambitious, it can be very easy to live life as a constant exercise in image management and performance, letting the world know (mostly online) what we're up to and how great it is (and we are).

This is a particular challenge for those whose work or ministry constantly demands performance of one kind of another, whether it is standing in front of a church to preach or in front of a classroom to teach or in front of a camera to present the news or in front of a patient's family to deliver information on their condition. Paul Tripp writes about the dangers of 'professional' ministry in particular:

Many pastors out there are seeking to lead and teach well, but it is simply not fuelled or directed by the devotion of their hearts to their saviour. Their Christianity is more an institutional discipline than a personal relationship. They are more drawn to ideas than to Jesus. They are more drawn to ministry success than personal growth.[34]

This challenge to purity of heart asks me what I would do for good even if no one ever saw or knew about it. How will I nurture the inner life of grace, listening to the still small voice of the One whom I have no need to impress? The heart is a person's innermost being, the seat of the will, so to be pure in heart is to be focused on the object of devotion: 'the pure in heart are those whose devotion to God is unalloyed.'[35]

Of course, no one is able to attain perfection in this regard and, as with all the other Beatitudes, this one has a forward-facing aspect. No one is completely pure of heart in our present earthly state, but one day in the fullness of the kingdom we will see God face to face. Therefore, if living the Beatitudes is embracing more deliberately now the future-oriented promises of God, one way in which we better appropriate this blessedness is by spending time before the face of God in the present, albeit a face that we now see 'through a glass darkly'. It is so easy to get caught up in the rat race of ambition and success, even in Christian circles, and to long therefore for that place of inner stillness and purity, alone with the audience of One, in prayer, solitude and worship, stripping away the things of the world and just being with God.

No agenda. No strategy. No plan.

Just be.

7 Extend hospitality

Blessed are the peacemakers, for they will be called children of God.

What does it look like to be called children of God? Children come to look, behave and act like their parents. To be a child of God is to be like God in his character. And one of God's attributes is that he is the God of peace (see 1 Corinthians 14.33; Romans 15.33; 2 Corinthians 13.11; Philippians 4.9; Hebrews 13.20).

If you are ambitious, you will be part of conflict, because that's just the way the world is. The way the kingdom is is not avoidance of conflict, but living well within it. Conflict can be creative and can herald new possibilities. As Jean Vanier writes:

Communities need tensions if they are to grow and deepen . . . . When everything is going well, when the community feels it is living successfully, its members tend to let their energies dissipate, and to listen less carefully to each other. Tensions bring people back to the reality of their helplessness; obliging them to spend more time in prayer and dialogue, to work patiently to overcome the crisis and refind lost unity; making them understand that the community is more than just a human reality, that it also needs the spirit of God if it is to live and deepen.[36]

This Beatitude, however, points to the fact that, when conflicts arise, there is a place for those who work for peace. Not simply peace *keepers*, but peace *makers*.

Some conflict arises because the ways of the kingdoms of this world are not the ways of the kingdom of God. The peacemakers are those who work to make the world more like the kingdom of our God. Peace in God's kingdom is not the absence of conflict but the renewal of right relationships in the whole of creation, so peacemaking is getting involved with the struggle to bring that about, as did Christ on the cross. We need to get our hands dirty and engage with the conflict in order to realize that true vision of peace for the whole cosmos for which we are destined, where, 'The wolf shall live with the lamb, the leopard shall lie down with the kid, the calf and the lion and the fatling together, and a little child shall lead them' (Isaiah 11.6).[37]

Peacemaking of this kind is very, very hard work. The truth of this came home to me listening to a friend speaking about his work in peace and reconciliation in South Sudan. Here is a country formed out of conflict, in which those who once united to defeat a common enemy have now fractured into factions and fighting. Joseph spends his life and his energy working with both sides to try to broker peace. The cost of this is written in his face and throughout his body. To be a peacemaker is to refuse to settle for quick solutions or appeasement or brush over the differences, but is walking the hard road of listening, learning, understanding and moving to new places where there are no winners and losers. 'Where others build walls, they painstakingly construct bridges.'[38]

Peacemaking is an act of hospitality. It involves engaging with the other, 'inviting the stranger into our world on his or her terms, not on ours'[39] and also a degree of confrontation, challenge, and the reconfiguring of views and ideas.

Nouwen points out the need for both hospitality (receptivity) and confrontation: 'Receptivity without confrontation leads to a bald neutrality that serves nobody. Confrontation without receptivity leads to an oppressive aggression which hurts everybody.'[40] To be a peacemaker of this kind demands a radical attitude to ambition since 'the absence of selfish ambition provides the only basis for this quality, which is particularly pleasing to God.'[41]

8 Be of good courage

Blessed are those who are persecuted for righteousness' sake, for theirs is the kingdom of heaven.

The kingdom of God and the kingdoms of this world are often in conflict. If we seek to live as citizens of the kingdom of God, and to inhabit the state of blessedness described in the Beatitudes, we are bound to arouse apathy at best, antipathy at worst. In the West, that antipathy mostly emerges as cynicism or indifference towards the Christian faith, and rarely outright hostility, but in other parts of the world this persecution takes a much more literal form.

The message of this final Beatitude is that leading according to the ways of Christ is more likely to make you unpopular than popular, less rather than more successful and more likely that your ambitions will be thwarted rather than fulfilled, at least in worldly terms. For those who have an active, lively and hungry approval monster, this is hard news to hear. We want to be popular, not persecuted. But this is a sobering reminder that when we follow the paths of the One who 'became sin who knew no sin' (2 Corinthians 5.21), our ambitions and successes will take on a very different hue. We're going to need to be people whose lives, ministry and work are shaped always and only by Christ, the King of his kingdom, in all its peculiar difference from the ways of the world that does not know or accept him (John 1.10–11).

This book has addressed issues of 'success' (even here in the final chapter I cannot resist the quotation marks) and growth, especially in the Church. As we long to see people come to know Jesus Christ, as we long to see the Church grow, as we dearly want to see people respond favourably to the gospel, the temptation before us will always be to make things more palatable, more relevant, more accessible, more acceptable. In some way this will be necessary. We do need to make sure that the gospel is presented in a way that is hearable, winsome and attractive. But we will also do well to remember that 66 per cent of the sower's seed fell on rocky and hostile ground, the gospel will always be an offence and a stumbling block to many, and we preach the gospel of the One who said, 'I have given them your word, and the world has hated them because they do not belong to the world, just as I do not belong to the world' (John 17.14). The temptation will always be to alter the message to conform to the ideas of this age about what is good for people and to forget the Creator King who made humankind and has showed us how to live. As Bonhoeffer said, 'the cross is not the terrible end to an otherwise God-fearing and happy life, but it meets us at the beginning of our communion with Christ. When Christ calls a man, he bids him come and die.'[42] You don't often see that as the strapline for a church, emblazoned on its website.

In acknowledging our own weakness and powerlessness to live like this, especially in the face of opposition, we know we rely only on the strength and purpose that comes from God's Holy Spirit. Yet, rely on it we can, and so we have confidence. When the going gets tough, we will find that 'this meeting point between our vulnerability and weakness on the one hand and divine strengthening on the other is what carries us through.'[43]

These days we hear much about the important quality of resilience. Resilience does not mean toughing it out, being able to cope, being hard-headed and cold-hearted. True resilience is the ability to bend and flex and grow, even through the hard times, and it is an important leadership quality. Rabbi Jonathan Sacks cites the example of Joseph, whose trust in God's purposes for his life gave him 'immense strength', which is 'what is what a leader needs if he [or she] is to dare greatly'. Sacks goes on to say:

> Whatever malice other people harbour against leaders – and the more successful they are, the more malice there is – if they can say "You intended to harm me, but God intended it for good," – they will survive, their strength intact, their energy undiminished.[44]

The Beatitudes weren't written for twenty-first-century leaders; they were spoken to a bunch of first-century followers of an itinerant preacher from Nazareth, sitting on a mountain somewhere in the middle of nowhere. But, incredibly, they resonate with so much of what we need to think about in these days of obsession with growth and ambition. They challenge us in the Church to be a community that again reflects the kingdom's character and promises exhibited by the One who spoke them. They help us to see our work, career, ambition – everything – in the light of the astoundingly humble vision they hold out to us. They spur us on to do all in our power to introduce others to the One who uttered these words, truly the most successful person who has ever lived by anyone's standards. What have these words to do with the power-obsessed culture of benchmarks and targets? What have they to say to a Church that seeks to grow and thrive and make a difference, and yet live like the kingdom is near? Bonhoeffer sums it up perfectly:

> Having reached the end of the beatitudes, we naturally ask if there is any place of this earth for the community which they describe. Clearly, there is one place, and only one, and that is where the poorest, meekest, and most sorely tried of all men is to be found – on the cross at Golgotha. The fellowship of the beatitudes is the fellowship of the Crucified. With him it has lost all, and with him it has found all. From the cross there comes the call 'blessed, blessed'.[45]

In all your ambitions and your successes and your failures, as you count and measure and plan and strategize and evaluate, as you climb ladders and seek promotions and work to grow whatever it is you are involved with, being rewarded and noticed, and asked to take on more responsibility and actually changing the world for God's kingdom, remember also to stay humble, to seek wholeness, show compassion, pursue rightness, address inequality, spend time alone with God, extend hospitality and be of good courage.

And may you be found in the great company of Blessed Ones in all your endeavours for his kingdom.

Go forth into the world in peace;
be of good courage;
hold fast that which is good;
render to no one evil for evil;
strengthen the fainthearted;
support the weak;
help the afflicted;
honour everyone;
love and serve the Lord,
rejoicing in the power of the Holy Spirit;
and the blessing of God Almighty,
the Father, the Son, and the Holy Spirit,
be among you and remain with you always. Amen. (BCP)

Notes

1 Success and failure

1 Churchill, *My Early Life*, p. 54.
2 Merton, *Love and Living*, p. 11.
3 <www.archbishopofcanterbury.org/priorities/evangelism-and-witness>
4 <www.churchofengland.org/about/renewal-and-reform>
5 <www.churchofengland.org/about/renewal-and-reform/more-about-renewal-reform>
6 Sons and Friends of the Clergy (since renamed the Clergy Support Trust) is a charity that exists for 'the 'relief and prevention of poverty or hardship' of the clergy of the Anglican Communion and their dependants, as well as 'the relief of illness and the promotion of health, whether physical or mental'. Its principal activity is to provide financial grants and other support to eligible beneficiaries in time of crisis or need. See < www.clergysupport.org.uk>.
7 Rudgard, 'Pressure to grow congregations leads to "clergy self-harm" says Christ Church Dean', *The Telegraph*.
8 *Church Times*, 'Church of England has prioritised leadership skills over theology, says Dean of Southwark'.
9 Hill, *Servant of All*.
10 *Concise Oxford English Dictionary* (12th edn) (Oxford University Press, 2011).
11 'In its earliest usages, then, success (and its corresponding verb) is something that can be positive or negative, and that largely depends on results or outcomes. In literature and culture, early modern success was something that happened as the consequence of something else' (Peterson and Martin, 'Tracing the origins of success: Implications for successful ageing', *The Gerontologist*).
12 Chesterton, 'The fallacy of success', pp. 19–24.
13 Edmondson, *The Fearless Organization*.
14 Edmondson, *The Fearless Organization*, p. 119.
15 Gregory the Great, 'The prologue', p. 2.
16 Brown, *Dare to Lead*, p. 43.

17 For example, Lord Green Steering Group (the Green Report).
18 The report, and discussion of it, can be found in, Alexander and Higton (eds), *Faithful Improvisation?*, p. 84.
19 Jones and Armstrong, *Resurrecting Excellence*, p. 135.
20 Jones and Armstrong, *Resurrecting Excellence*, p. 39.
21 A phrase used by Brené Brown in various of her works.
22 Cook, 'A few thoughts on five years of succeeding and failing at pioneering'.
23 Jones and Armstrong, *Resurrecting Excellence*, p. 21.
24 Aristotle, *Nicomachean Ethics*.
25 Teaching Excellence Framework page on the Office for Students website; Office for Students, 'What is the TEF?'
26 Woolley and Robinson-Garcia, 'The 2014 REF results show only a very weak relationship between excellence in research and achieving societal impact'.
27 Tripp, *Dangerous Calling*, p. 142.

2 Climbing

1 Shakespeare, *Macbeth*, Act 2, Scene 2.
2 Spurgeon, *The Check Book of Faith*; quoted in Harvey, *Rescuing Ambition*, p. 118.
3 Wilson, 'When did ambition become a dirty word in Bristol?'.
4 Banksy, quoted in Wilson.
5 Hill, *Servant of All*, p. 134.
6 The Greek word is *episkopos*, which some translations render 'overseer' or 'leader' instead of 'bishop'.
7 Merriam-Webster online dictionary.
8 William Shakespeare, *Julius Caesar*, Act III, Scene II.
9 Bradbury, *Stepping into Grace*, p. 23.
10 Bradbury, *Stepping into Grace*, drawing on the work of Joseph B. Soltoveitchik, *The Lonely Man of Faith* (London: Random House, 2006).
11 Bradbury, *Stepping into Grace*, p. 21.
12 Bradbury, *Stepping into Grace*, p. 22.
13 'Thus I make it my ambition to proclaim the good news, not where Christ has already been named, so that I do not build on someone

else's foundation, but as it is written, "those who have never been told of him shall see, and those who have never heard of him shall understand"' (Romans 15.20).

14 Hill, *Servant of All*, p. 143.

15 Hill, *Servant of All*, p. 141.

16 Monbiot, 'As robots take our jobs, we need something else. I know what that is'.

17 Burton, 'Is ambition good or bad?'

18 Cited in Fels, 'Do women lack ambition?', p. 23.

19 Smith, *Desiring the Kingdom*.

20 Smith, *Desiring the Kingdom*, p. 47.

21 Smith, *Desiring the Kingdom*, p. 49.

22 Smith, *Desiring the Kingdom*, p. 51.

23 Smith, *Desiring the Kingdom*, p. 51.

24 Wells, *What Anglicans Believe*, p. 79.

25 Bradbury, *Stepping Into Grace*, p. 23.

26 Fairley, 'I may be successful, but whatever you do, don't call me an "ambitious" woman'.

27 Harrison Warren, 'Who's afraid of her own authority?'

28 Fels, 'Do Women Lack Ambition?', p. 25.

29 Lord Green Steering Group (the Green Report), p. 23.

30 Smith, *Desiring the Kingdom*, p. 17.

31 Neuhaus, *Freedom for Ministry*, p. 219.

32 Tripp, *Dangerous Calling*, p. 173.

33 Jones and Armstrong, *Resurrecting Excellence*, p. 63.

34 Jones and Armstrong, *Resurrecting Excellence*, p. 65.

35 A classic definition of theological reflection comes from Killen and de Beer: 'the discipline of exploring our individual and corporate experience in conversation with the wisdom of a religious heritage', *The Art of Theological Reflection*, p. viii.

36 Jones and Armstrong, *Resurrecting Excellence*, p. 69.

3 Counting

1 Herbert, 'Good Friday', p. 59.

2 Welby, Archbishop of Canterbury, in interview with Madeleine Davies for the *Church Times*.

3 *Brexit: The Uncivil War*, first shown 7 January 2019, Channel 4 TV.

4 Williams, 'Surgeon David Grant: "These are human beings, not numbers"'.

5 Bradbury, *Stepping Into Grace*, p. 29.

6 Valler, *Using Measurement Well*, p. 3.

7 Cameron, *Informal Sociology*, p. 13.

8 Valler, *Using Measurement Well*, p. 23.

9 Welby, *Dethroning Mammon*, p. 37.

10 Valler, *Using Measurement Well*, p. 6.

11 'Most key measures of attendance fell by between 10 per cent and 20 per cent from 2007 to 2017. See Church of England, 'Statistics for mission, 2017'.

12 Goodhew, 'Transformed, not conformed', p. 236.

13 Paul, 'What are the church attendance statistics telling us?'

14 This is often translated as 'to shake' – 'He stopped and shook the earth' (NRSV), 'He stood, and shook the earth' (NIV) – but the Hebrew verb *mdd* is better translated as 'measured', along with related nouns, *middah* I (measure) or *middah* II (tax) and *memad* (measurement).

15 McGrath, 'Theology, eschatology and church growth', p. 97.

16 'The Marketable Revolution', *The Simple Way Online Newsletter*, March 2006; quoted in Sine, *The New Conspirators*, p. 23.

17 Spencer, *Growing and Flourishing*, p. 51.

18 Goodhew, *Towards a Theology of Church Growth*, p. 34.

19 Sacks, *Lessons in Leadership*, p. 184.

20 Sacks, 'What counts?', p. 3.

21 Sacks, 'What counts?', p. 3.

22 Rashi to Num 1.1, quoted in Sacks, *Lessons in Leadership*, p. 183.

23 Sacks, *Lessons in Leadership*, p. 185

24 Sacks, *Lessons in Leadership*, p. 186.

25 The Yad Vashem website states, 'There is no precise figure for the number of Jews killed in the Holocaust.' The figure of around 6 million is most often used.

26 Holocaust Memorial Day Trust, 'We release research to mark Holocaust Memorial Day 2019'.

27 De Pree, *Leadership Is an Art*, p. 11.

28 Valler, *Using Measurement Well*, p. 28.

29 Rendle, *Doing the Math of Mission*, p. 17.

30 Rendle, *Doing the Math of Mission*, p. 14.

31 Rendle, *Doing the Math of Mission*, p. 43.

32 Rendle, *Doing the Math of Mission*, p. 17.

33 Rendle, *Doing the Math of Mission*, p. 22.

34 Rendle, *Doing the Math of Mission*, p. 11.

35 Pearce, 'Want to improve the chances of funding your policy priority?'

36 Pearce, 'The poverty of targetism'.

37 Williams, 'Surgeon David Grant: "These are human beings, not numbers"'.

38 Bonhoeffer, 'No rusty swords', pp. 216–17.

39 Rudgard, 'Pressure to grow congregations leads to "clergy self-harm" says Christ Church Dean'.

40 Peterson, *Practice Resurrection*, p. 244.

41 McGrath, 'Theology, eschatology and church growth', p. 93.

42 McGrath, 'Theology, eschatology and church growth', p. 101.

43 McGrath, 'Theology, eschatology and church growth', p. 103.

44 Valler, *Using Measurement Well*, p. 27.

45 Valler, *Using Measurement Well*, p. 24.

46 Valler, *Using Measurement Well*, p. 24.

47 General Synod, 'Resourcing ministerial education in the Church of England', p. 1 [emphasis mine].

48 See, for example, General Synod, 'Resourcing ministerial education in the Church of England', p. 3: 'It is not clear that the present arrangements ensure value for money'.

49 Macmath, 'Interview: Ian McFarland'.

50 Alexander and Higton, *Faithful Improvisation?*, p. 22.

51 For a fuller discussion, see Wenham, *The Parables of Jesus*, p. 48.

4 Comparing

1 Oliver, 'The summer day'.

2 Lightbown, 'Talking of leadership and governance'.

3 All about Madonna, 'Madonna interview: Vanity Fair'.

4 Dolan, 'The money, job, marriage myth'.

5 Saunders, 'Why do evangelists exaggerate?'

6 Nouwen, *In the Name of Jesus*, p. 38.

7 Lord Green Steering Group (the Green Report).

8 Petriglieri and Petriglieri, 'The talent curse'.

9 Beach, *Gifted to Lead*, p. 33.

10 For example, Eagly and Johnson found that women's leadership styles were more democratic and participative than men's ('Gender and leadership style'), Eagly, Johannesen-Schmidt and van Engen found that women leaders were more collaborative and more likely to aim to increase the self-worth of others than were male leaders ('Transformational, transactional, and laissez-faire leadership styles', and Mckinsey & Company found that women were more people-based and set clearer expectations and rewards than men (McKinsey & Company, 'Women matter 2').

11 Zenger and Folkman found that women are rated more competent in taking initiative, practising self-development, integrity and honesty and driving for results than men ('Are women better leaders than men?').

12 Coleman, *7 Deadly Sins of Women in Leadership*, p. 204.

13 Lord Green Steering Group (the Green Report).

14 Keillor, *Lake Wobegon Days*, p. 263.

15 Ortberg, 'Breaking the approval addiction'.

16 A phrase originally attributed to John Wimber.

17 Merton, *New Seeds of Contemplation*, p. 190.

18 Marshall, *The Epistles of John*, p. 90.

19 Diocese of Bristol, 'Ministerial development review'.

20 Crouch says that good leadership requires both authority – 'the capacity for meaningful action' – and vulnerability – 'exposure to meaningful risk.' Authority without vulnerability leads to exploiting others. Vulnerability without authority can lead to our risking very little, but also having little impact, influence or capacity for action (Crouch, *Strong and Weak*, p. 35).

21 Sermon 387.2, quoted in Beeley, *Leading God's People*, p. 127.

22 Jones and Armstrong. *Resurrecting Excellence*, p. 92.

23 Nouwen, *In the Name of Jesus*, p. 62.

24 Tripp, *Dangerous Calling*, p.157.

25 Cited in Jones and Armstrong, *Resurrecting Excellence*, p. 43.

26 Crouch, 'It's time to reckon with celebrity power'.

27 Nouwen, *In the Name of Jesus*, p. 80.

28 Lewis, *Mere Christianity*, p. 128.

29 Harrison Warren, 'Who's afraid of her own authority?'

30 Gladwell, *Outliers*, Chapter 7.

31 Darzi, 'Surgeons do make mistakes – time to reboot the surgery checklist'.

5 Leadership in the image of the Trinity

1 Tweet by BBC political correspondent Nick Robinson in the days following the 2016 Brexit vote.

2 *Brexit: The Battle for Britain*, first shown 25 August 2016 on BBC2 TV.

3 May, *The Express*.

4 Weber, *Economy and Society*.

5 A theme developed in Tomlin, *The Widening Circle*.

6 'And Jesus came and said to them, "All authority in heaven and on earth has been given to me. Go therefore and make disciples of all nations, baptizing them in the name of the Father and of the Son and of the Holy Spirit, and teaching them to obey everything that I have commanded you"' (Matthew 28.18–20).

7 Neuhaus, *Freedom for Ministry*, p. 71.

8 Neuhaus, *Freedom for Ministry*, p. 71.

9 Hoyle, *The Pattern of Our Calling*, p. 17.

10 Andrew Nunn, sermon preached at the Memorial Service for the Very Reverend David Edwards, Tuesday, 27 November, 2018.

11 Stackhouse, *Primitive Piety*, p. 110.

12 Bradbury, *Stepping Into Grace*, p. 25.

13 Thistleton, *1 Corinthians*, p. 45.

14 Bonhoeffer, *Meditations on the Cross*, p. 54.

15 Bonhoeffer, *Meditations on the Cross*, p. 54.

16 'Their special dark privilege is to be pain bearers, keeping vigil with a damaged world until God finally puts all the world to rights in his new creation' (Pritchard, *The Life and Work of a Priest*, p. 66).

17 Jones and Armstrong, *Resurrecting Excellence*, p. 39.

18 Weber, *Economy and Society*, p. 215.

19 Anderson, *The Shape of Practical Theology*, p. 105.

20 Jones and Armstrong, *Resurrecting Excellence*, p. 133.

21 Purportedly said by Napoleon.

22 Lewis, *The Screwtape Letters*, p. 76.

23 Lewis, *The Screwtape Letters*, p. 75.

24 Thomas, 'The Bright Field'.

25 Wright,. *How God Became King*, p. 198.

26 Jones and Armstrong, *Resurrecting Excellence*, p. 21.

27 Jones and Armstrong, *Resurrecting Excellence*, p. 123.

28 Dykstra, *Keys to Excellence*, quoted in Jones and Armstrong, *Resurrecting Excellence*, p. 125.

29 Deuteronomy 30.15,19, cited in Sacks, *Lessons in Leadership*, pp. 263–7.

30 Sacks, *Lessons in Leadership*, p. 261.

31 Jones and Armstrong, *Resurrecting Excellence*, p. 133.

32 Hill, *Servant of All*, p. 138.

33 Ibarra and Obodaru, 'Women and the vision thing', p. 53.

34 Ibarra and Obodaru, 'Women and the vision thing', p. 58.

6 Key spiritual dispositions for ambitious people

1 Wright, *Matthew for Everyone*, p. 34.

2 France, *The Gospel of Matthew*, p. 161.

3 McKnight, *The Sermon on the Mount*, p. 32.

4 For example, Psalm 1.1 – 'Happy (blessed, flourishing) are those who do not follow the advice of the wicked, or take the path that sinners tread' – and Isaiah 32.20 – 'Happy (blessed, flourishing) will you be who sow beside every stream, who let the ox and the donkey range freely' – cited in Pennington, *The Sermon on the Mount and Human Flourishing*.

5 Pennington, *The Sermon on the Mount and Human Flourishing*, p. 156.

6 Wright, *Matthew for Everyone*, p. 38.

7 Willard, *The Divine Conspiracy*, p. 121.

8 Pennington, *The Sermon on the Mount and Human Flourishing*, p. 160.

9 Jones and Armstrong, *Resurrecting Excellence*, p. 57. See also France, 'This Godlike character in its entirely should be

progressively seen in all true disciples, because only where it is found is the kingdom of heaven, God's control, really effective' (*Matthew*, p. 111).

10 Willimon, 'Looking like fools (1 Cor. 1–23)', p. 261.

11 Friendship, *Enfolded in Christ*, p. 40.

12 Donald Trump, in an interview on '60 Minutes', CBS News, 2 February 2016.

13 Keller, *The Freedom of Self-Forgetfulness*.

14 Jones and Armstrong, *Resurrecting Excellence*, p. 42.

15 Williams, *The Merciful Humility of God*, p. 148.

16 Tomlin, *The Widening Circle*, p. 145.

17 Collins, *Good to Great*, p. 39.

18 Edmondson, *The Fearless Organization*, p. 114.

19 Flood, 'JK Rowling's writing advice: be a Gryffindor'.

20 Williams, *The Merciful Humility of God*, p. 149.

21 Hare, *Matthew*, p. 36. See also Pennington, *The Sermon on the Mount and Human Flourishing*, p. 60.

22 Schweizer, *The Good News According to Matthew*, p. 90.

23 I am grateful to Dr Justin Stratis for this insight, gained from a sermon he preached at Trinity College Chapel as part of a series on the Beatitudes.

24 Bridge, *Ambition*, p. 167.

25 Bridge, *Ambition*, p. 142.

26 Augustine of Hippo, *Our Lord's Sermon on the Mount*, p. 4.

27 France, *The Gospel of Matthew*, p. 94.

28 Pennington, *The Sermon on the Mount and Human Flourishing*, p. 91.

29 France, *The Gospel of Matthew*, p. 111.

30 Schweizer, *The Good News According to Matthew*, p. 90.

31 Hare, *Matthew*, p. 40. See, for example, Matthew 18.23–25 and Luke 6.36.

32 Hare, *Matthew*, p. 40.

33 Augustine of Hippo, *Our Lord's Sermon on the Mount*, p. 8.

34 Tripp, *Dangerous Calling*, p. 183.

35 Hare, *Matthew*, p. 41.

36 Vanier, *Community and Growth*, p. 120.

37 I am grateful to Dr Helen Collins for these insights.

38 Hare, *Matthew*, p. 43.

39 Nouwen, *Reaching Out*, p. 98.

40 Nouwen, *Reaching Out*, p. 72.

41 France, *The Gospel of Matthew*, p. 111.

42 Bonhoeffer, *The Cost of Discipleship*, p. 99.

43 Sermon preached by Professor John Nolland in Trinity College Chapel.

44 Sacks, *Lessons in Leadership*, p. 58.

45 Bonhoeffer, *The Cost of Discipleship*, pp. 113–14.

Bibliography

Alexander, L. and Higton, M. (eds), *Faithful Improvisation?: Theological reflections on church leadership* (London: Church House Publishing, 2016).

All about Madonna, 'Madonna interview: Vanity Fair' (available online at: <https://allaboutmadonna.com/madonna-interviews/madonna-interview-vanity-fair-april-1991/4>, accessed 15 January 2019).

Anderson, R. *The Shape of Practical Theology* (Downers Grove, IL: InterVarsity Press, 2001).

Archbishop of Canterbury (available online at: <www.archbishopofcanterbury.org/priorities/evangelism-and-witness>, accessed 12 January 2019).

Aristotle, *Nicomachean Ethics*, II vi 15, H. Rackham (trans.) (Cambridge, MA: Harvard University Press, 1934).

Augustine of Hippo, *Our Lord's Sermon on the Mount*, The Reverend William Findlay (trans.) (Aeterna Press, 2014).

Banksy, *Banging Your Head Against a Brick Wall* (London: Weapons of Mass Destruction, 2001).

Beach, N., *Gifted to Lead: The art of leading as a woman in the Church* (Grand Rapids, MI: Zondervan, 2014).

Beeley, C. A., *Leading God's People: Wisdom from the early Church for today* (Grand Rapids, MI: Eerdmans, 2012).

Bonhoeffer, D., *Meditations on the Cross*, Manfred Weber (ed.), Douglas W. Stott (English trans.) (Louisville, KY: Westminster John Knox Press, 1998).

Bonhoeffer, D., 'No rusty swords: Letters, lectures and notes 1928–1936', in, *The Collected Works of Dietrich Bonhoeffer*, Volume I (New York: Harper & Row, 1965).

Bonhoeffer, D., *The Cost of Discipleship* (New York: Touchstone, Simon & Schuster, 2018).

Bradbury, P., *Stepping into Grace* (Abingdon: Bible Reading Fellowship, 2016).

Bridge, R., *Ambition: Why it's good to want more and how to get it* (Chichester: Capstone, John Wiley & Sons, 2016).

Brown, B., *Dare to Lead: Daring greatly and rising strong at work* (London: Vermilion, 2018).

Burton, N., 'Is ambition good or bad?: The psychology and philosophy of ambition', *Psychology Today*, 16 November 2014 (available online at: <www.psychologytoday.com/gb/blog/hide-and-seek/201411/is-ambition-good-or-bad>, accessed 12 February 2019).

Cameron, W. B., *Informal Sociology: A casual introduction to sociological thinking* (New York: Random House,1963).

Chesterton, G. K., 'The fallacy of success', in, *All Things Considered* (Philadelphia, PA: Dufour Editions, 1969).

Church of England, 'Renewal and reform' (available online at: <www.churchofengland.org/about/renewal-and-reform>, accessed 1 November 2018).

Church of England, 'Theological reflections' (available online at: <www.churchofengland.org/about/renewal-and-reform/more-about-renewal-reform>, accessed 1 February 2019).

Church of England, 'Statistics for mission, 2017' (available online at www.churchofengland.org/sites/default/files/2018-11/2017StatisticsForMission.pdf>, accessed 13 February 2019).

Church Times, 'Church of England has prioritised leadership skills over theology, says Dean of Southwark', *Church Times*, 30 November 2018 (available online at <www.churchtimes.co.uk/articles/2018/30-november/news/uk/church-of-england-has-prioritised-leadership-skills-over-theology-says-dean-of-southwark>, accessed 15 January 2019).

Churchill, W., *My Early Life* (new edition) (London: Eland, 2000).

Coleman, K., *7 Deadly Sins of Women in Leadership: Overcome self-defeating behaviour in work and ministry* (Birmingham: Next Leadership, 2010).

Collins, J., *Good to Great* (London: Random House, 2001).

Cook, R., 'A few thoughts on five years of succeeding and failing at pioneering' (available online at: <https://medium.com/@ryancook_53468/a-few-thoughts-on-five-years-of-succeeding-and-failing-at-pioneering-71df057a3c96>, accessed 17 February 2019)

Crouch, A., *Strong and Weak: Embracing a life of love, risk and true flourishing* (Downers Grove, IL: InterVarsity Press, 2016).

Crouch, A., 'It's time to reckon with celebrity power', *Gospel Coalition*, 24 March 2018 (available online at: <www.thegospelcoalition.org/article/time-reckon-celebrity-power>, accessed 15 February 2019).

Darzi, A., 'Surgeons do make mistakes – time to reboot the surgery checklist', *The Guardian*, 31 January 2019 (available online at <www.theguardian.com/commentisfree/2019/jan/31/surgeons-make-mistakes-surgery-checklist-operation>, accessed 14 February 2019).

Diocese of Bristol, 'Ministerial development review' (available online at: <www.bristol.anglican.org/ministerial-development-review>, accessed 1 February 2019).

Dolan, P., 'The money, job, marriage myth: Are you happy yet?', *The Guardian*, 6 January 2019 (available online at: <www.theguardian.com/books/2019/jan/06/happiness-index-wellbeing-survey-uk-population-paul-dolan-happy-ever-after>, accessed 10 January 2019).

De Pree, M., *Leadership Is an Art* (New York: Currency, 2004).

Eagly, A. H., and Johnson, B. T., 'Gender and leadership style: A meta-analysis', 1990 (available online at: <www.scholars.northwestern.edu/en/publications/gender-and-leadership-style-a-meta-analysis-2>, accessed 15 February 2019).

Eagly, A. H., Johannesen-Schmidt, M. C. and van Engen, M. L., 'Transformational, transactional, and laissez-faire leadership styles: A meta-analysis comparing women and men', *Psychological Bulletin*, 2003, 129(4), pp. 569–91.

Edmondson, A. C., *The Fearless Organization: Creating psychological safety in the workplace for learning, innovation and growth* (Hoboken, NJ: John Wiley & Sons, 2019).

Fairley, J., 'I may be successful, but whatever you do, don't call me an "ambitious" woman. It's insulting', *The Telegraph*, 9 October 2013 (available online at: <www.telegraph.co.uk/women/womens-business/10366053/Ambition-is-a-dirty-word-I-may-be-successful-but-whatever-you-do-dont-call-me-an-ambitious-woman.-Its-insulting.html>, accessed 13 February 2019).

Fels, A., 'Do women lack ambition?', in, *On Women and Leadership* (Cambridge, MA: Harvard Business School, 2019).

Flood, A., 'JK Rowling's writing advice: Be a Gryffindor', *The Guardian*, 8 January 2019 (available online at: <www.theguardian.com/books/booksblog/2019/jan/08/jk-rowlings-writing-advice-be-a-gryffindor>, accessed 9 January 2019).

France, D., *The Gospel of Matthew* (The New International Commentary on the New Testament) (Grand Rapids, MI: Eerdmans, 2007).

France, R. T., *Matthew* (Tyndale New Testament Commentaries) (Leicester: IVP, 1985).

Friendship, J. F., *Enfolded in Christ: The inner life of a priest* (Norwich: Canterbury Press, 2018).

General Synod, 'Resourcing ministerial education in the Church of England: A report from the Task Group', GS 1979, 2015 (available online at: <www.churchofengland.org/sites/default/files/2017-12/gs%201979%20-%20resourcing%20ministerial%20education%20task%20group%20report.pdf>, accessed 15 February 2019).

Gladwell, M., *Outliers: The story of success* (London: Penguin, 2008).

Goodhew, D., 'Transformed, not conformed: Towards a theology of church growth', in, D. Goodhew (ed.), *Towards a Theology of Church Growth* (Ashgate Contemporary Ecclesiology Series) (Abingdon: Routledge, 2015).

Gregory the Great, 'The prologue' from *The Book of Pastoral Rule* (Aeterna Press, 2016).

Hare, D. R. A., *Matthew: Interpretation: A Bible commentary for teaching and preaching* (London: John Knox Press, 1993).

Harrison Warren, T., 'Who's afraid of her own authority?', *Christianity Today* (available online at: <www.christianitytoday.

com/women/2016/september/women-vulnerability-and-leadership.html>, accessed 19 February 2019).

Harvey, D., *Rescuing Ambition* (Wheaton, IL: Crossway, 2010).

Herbert, G., 'Good Friday', in, *The English Poems of George Herbert*, C. A. Patrides (ed.) (London: Everyman/J. M. Dent, 1974), p. 59.

Hill, C. C., *Servant of All: Status, ambition, and the way of Jesus* (Grand Rapids, MI: Eerdmans, 2016).

Holocaust Memorial Day Trust, 'We release research to mark Holocaust Memorial Day 2019' (available online at: <www.hmd.org.uk/news/we-release-research-to-mark-holocaust-memorial-day-2019>, accessed 28 January 2019).

Hoyle, D., *The Pattern of Our Calling* (London: SCM Press, 2016).

Ibarra, H. and Obodaru, O., 'Women and the vision thing', in, *On Women and Leadership* (Harvard Business Review Press, 2018) p. 53.

Jones, G. and Armstrong, K. C., *Resurrecting Excellence: Shaping faithful Christian ministry* (Grand Rapids, MI: Eerdmans, 2006).

Keillor, G., *Lake Wobegon Days* (London: Faber & Faber, 1986).

Keller, T., *The Freedom of Self-Forgetfulness* (Leyland, Lancashire: 10Publishing, 2012).

Killen, P. O. and de Beer, J., *The Art of Theological Reflection* (New York: Crossroad Publishing, 1994).

Lewis, C. S., *Mere Christianity* (1952; New York: Harper Collins, 2001).

Lewis, C. S., *The Screwtape Letters: Letters from a senior to a junior devil* (London: Fount Paperbacks, 2012).

Lightbown, A., 'Talking of leadership and governance' (available online at: <https://theore0.wordpress.com/2018/03/20/talking-of-leadership-and-governance>, accessed 15 February 2019).

Lord Green Steering Group, 'Talent management for future leaders and leadership development for bishops and deans: A new approach' (the Green Report), September 2014 (available online at: <www.thinkinganglicans.org.uk/uploads/TalentManagement.pdf>, accessed 12 February 2019).

Marshall, I. H., *The Epistles of John* (New International Commentary on the New Testament) (Grand Rapids, MI: Eerdmans 1995).

May, T., 'As Britain faces most momentous moment since the War Theresa May writes for the Express', *The Express*, 13 January 2019 (available online at: <www.express.co.uk/news/politics/1071241/Theresa-May-latest-Brexit-news-EU-meaningful-vote-express>, accessed 4 February 2019).

McGrath, A., 'Theology, eschatology and church growth', in, Goodhew, D. (ed.), *Towards a Theology of Church Growth* (Ashgate Contemporary Ecclesiology Series) (Abingdon: Routledge, 2015).

McKinsey & Company, 'Women Matter 2: Female leadership, a competitive edge for the future', 2009 (available online at: <www.mckinsey.com/~/media/mckinsey/business%20functions/organization/our%20insights/women%20matter/women_matter_oct2008_english.ashx>, accessed 15 February 2019).

McKnight, S., *The Sermon on the Mount* (The Story of God Bible Commentary) (Grand Rapids, MI: Zondervan, 2013).

Macmath T. H., 'Interview: Ian McFarland, Regius Professor of Divinity, Cambridge', *Church Times*, 20 April 2018.

Merton, T., *Love and Living*, N. M. Burton Stone and Brother P. Hart (eds) (New York: Farrar, Straus & Giroux, 1979).

Merton, T., *New Seeds of Contemplation* (New York: New Direction, 1972).

Monbiot, G., 'As robots take our jobs, we need something else. I know what that is', *The Guardian*, 7 February 2018 (available online at: <www.theguardian.com/commentisfree/2018/feb/07/robots-jobs-salaried-work-society-unpaid-george-monbiot>, accessed 19 February 2019).

Neuhaus, R., *Freedom for Ministry* (2nd revd edn) (Grand Rapids, MI: Eerdmans, 1992).

Nouwen, H., *In the Name of Jesus* (London: Darton, Longman & Todd, 1989).

Nouwen, H., *Reaching Out: The three movements of the spiritual life* (London: Fount, 1996).

Office for Students, 'What is the TEF?' (available online at <www.officeforstudents.org.uk/advice-and-guidance/teaching/what-is-the-tef/>, accessed 8 January 2019).

Oliver, M., 'The summer day', in *House of Light: Poems by Mary Oliver* (Boston, MA: Beacon Press, 1992).

Ortberg, J., 'Breaking the approval addiction', *Christianity Today* (available online at: <www.christianitytoday.com/pastors/leadership-books/prayerpersonalgrowth/lclead04-15.html>, accessed 15 February 2019).

Paul, I., 'What are the church attendance statistics telling us?', Psephizo, 10 December 2018 (available online at: www.psephizo.com/life-ministry/what-are-the-church-attendance-statistics-telling-us>, accessed 19 January 2019).

Pearce, W., 'The poverty of targetism: Five years of the UK Climate Change Act', *The Guardian*, 26 November 2013 (available online at: <www.theguardian.com/science/2013/nov/26/the-poverty-of-targetism-five-years-of-the-uk-climate-change-act>, accessed 21 February 2019).

Pennington, J. T., *The Sermon on the Mount and Human Flourishing: A theological commentary* (Grand Rapids, MI: Baker Academic, 2018).

Peterson, E., *Practice Resurrection: A conversation on growing up in Christ* (Grand Rapids, MI: Eerdmans, 2010).

Peterson, N. M. and Martin, P., 'Tracing the origins of success: Implications for successful ageing', *The Gerontologist*, 2015, 55(1), pp. 5–13.

Petriglieri, J. and Petriglieri, G., 'The talent curse', *Harvard Business Review*, May/June 2017 (available online at: <https://hbr.org/2017/05/the-talent-curse>, accessed 14 February 2019).

Pritchard, J., *The Life and Work of a Priest* (London: SPCK, 2007).

Rendle, G., *Doing the Math of Mission: Fruits, faithfulness, and metrics* (Lanham, MD: Rowman & Littlefield, 2014).

Robinson, N., 'WANTED: For small country heading in unknown direction at dangerous time LEADERSHIP. Applicants need to be available to start immediately', Tweet, 26 June 2016 (@bbcnickrobinson).

Rudgard, O., 'Pressure to grow congregations leads to "clergy self-harm" says Christ Church Dean', *The Telegraph*, 14 November 2017 (available online at: <www.telegraph.co.uk/news/2017/11/14/pressure-grow-congregations-leads-clergy-self-harm-says-christ>, accessed 15 February 2019).

Sacks, J., *Lessons in Leadership: A weekly reading of the Jewish Bible* (Jerusalem: Maggid Books, 2015).

Sacks, J., 'What counts?', in, *Orthodox Union Torah*, 27 June 2018 (available online at: <www.ou.org/torah/parsha/rabbi-sacks-on-parsha/what_counts>, 13 February 2019).

Saunders, M., 'Why do evangelists exaggerate?', *Christianity Today*, 10 July 2017 (available online at: <www.christiantoday.com/article/why-do-evangelists-exaggerate/110561.htm>, accessed 15 February 2019).

Schweizer, E. T., *The Good News According to Matthew* (London: SPCK, 1976).

Sine, T., *The New Conspirators: Creating the future one mustard seed at a time* (Downers Grove, IL: InterVarsity Press, 2008).

Smith, J. K. A., *Desiring the Kingdom: Worship, worldview, and cultural formation* (Grand Rapids, MI: Baker Academic, 2009).

Southwark Cathedral, 'Memorial service for The Very Revd David Edwards' (available online at: <https://cathedral.southwark.anglican.org/worship-and-music/worship/sermons-from-special-services/memorial-service-for-the-very-revd-david-edwards>, accessed 1 February 2019).

Spencer, S., *Growing and Flourishing: The ecology of Church growth* (London: SCM Press, 2019).

Spurgeon, C., *The Check Book of Faith: Precious promises for daily readings* (Fearn, Ross-shire: Christian Focus Publications, 1996).

Stackhouse, I., *Primitive Piety: A journey from suburban mediocrity to passionate Christianity* (Milton Keynes: Paternoster, 2012).

Thistleton, A. C., *1 Corinthians: A shorter exegetical and pastoral commentary* (Grand Rapids, MI: Eerdmans, 2011).

Thomas, R. S., 'The bright field', in *Selected Poems* (London: Penguin, 2004), p. 114.

Tomlin, G., *The Widening Circle: Priesthood as God's way of blessing the world* (London: SPCK, 2014).

Tripp, P. D., *Dangerous Calling: The unique challenges of pastoral ministry* (Nottingham: IVP, 2012).

Valler, P., *Using Measurement Well: Encouraging a culture of human flourishing*, L15 (Nottingham: Grove, 2014).

Vanier, J., *Community and Growth* (London: Darton, Longman & Todd, 2006).

Weber, M., *Economy and Society: An outline of interpretive sociology*, Volume 1, Guenther Roth and Claus Wittich (eds) (Berkeley, CA: University of California Press, 1978).

Welby, J., *Dethroning Mammon* (London: Bloomsbury Continuum, 2016).

Welby, J. in interview with Madeleine Davies, 'To the sea again', *Church Times*, 22 November 2018 (available online at: <www.churchtimes.co.uk/articles/2018/23-november/features/features/interview-with-justin-welby-at-home-at-sea>, accessed 27 November 2018>).

Wells, S., *What Anglicans Believe* (Norwich: Canterbury Press 2011).

Wenham, D., *The Parables of Jesus* (Downers Grove, IL: InterVarsity Press, 1989).

Willard, D., *The Divine Conspiracy: Rediscovering our hidden life in God* (London: Harper Collins, 2014).

Williams, J., *The Merciful Humility of God* (London: Bloomsbury Continuum, 2018).

Williams, S., 'Surgeon David Grant: "These are human beings, not numbers"', *The Times*, 3 April 2018 (available online at: <www.thetimes.co.uk/article/david-grant-these-are-human-beings-not-numbers-wjbbc809d>, accessed 15 February 2019).

Willimon, W., 'Looking like fools (1 Cor. 1–23)', *Christian Century*, 10 March 1982, p. 261.

Wilson, K., 'When did ambition become a dirty word in Bristol?', *The Spectator*, 29 November 2014 (available online at: <www.spectator.co.uk/2014/11/whats-the-matter-with-bristol>, accessed 19 February 2019).

Woolley, R. and Robinson-Garcia, N., 'The 2014 REF results show only a very weak relationship between excellence in research and achieving societal impact', London School of Economics Impact Blog (available online at: <http://blogs.lse.ac.uk/impactofsocialsciences/2017/07/19/what-do-the-2014-ref-results-tell-us-about-the-relationship-between-excellent-research-and-societal-impact>, accessed 31 January 2019).

Wright, N. T., *How God Became King: Getting to the heart of the Gospels* (London: SPCK, 2012).

Wright, T., *Matthew for Everyone: Part 1, Chapters 1–15* (London: SPCK, 2002).

Yad Vashem (available at <www.yadvashem.org>, accessed 11 April 2019).

Zenger, J. and Folkman, J., 'Are women better leaders than men?', *Harvard Business Review*, 15 March 2012 (available online at: <https://hbr.org/2012/03/a-study-in-leadership-women-do>, accessed 15 February 2019).